THE OLD TESTAMENT

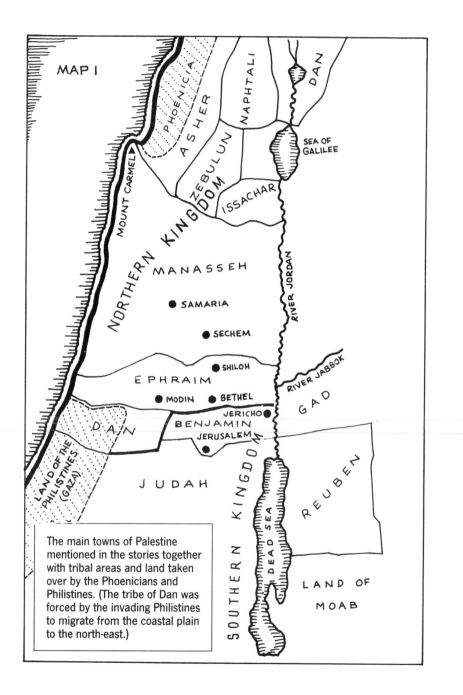

MAP I

PHOENICIA

ASHER

NAPHTALI

DAN

ZEBULUN

NORTHERN KINGDOM

MOUNT CARMEL

ISSACHAR

SEA OF
GALILEE

MANASSEH

● SAMARIA

● SECHEM

RIVER JORDAN

EPHRAIM

● SHILOH

RIVER JABBOK

● MODIN   ● BETHEL

GAD

JERICHO ●

BENJAMIN

JERUSALEM ●

D A N

LAND OF THE
PHILISTINES:
(GAZA).

JUDAH

SOUTHERN KINGDOM

DEAD SEA

REUBEN

LAND OF

MOAB

The main towns of Palestine
mentioned in the stories together
with tribal areas and land taken
over by the Phoenicians and
Philistines. (The tribe of Dan was
forced by the invading Philistines
to migrate from the coastal plain
to the north-east.)

BIBLE STORIES

FOR

CLASSROOM AND ASSEMBLY

THE OLD TESTAMENT

Jack G. Priestley
Principal, Westhill College, Birmingham

With Ideas for Exploring Further by

Angela M. Horton
Lecturer in Primary Education, Exeter University

RMEP

RELIGIOUS AND MORAL EDUCATION PRESS

Religious and Moral Education Press
An imprint of Chansitor Publications Ltd,
a wholly owned subsidiary of Hymns Ancient & Modern Ltd
St Mary's Works, St Mary's Plain
Norwich, Norfolk NR3 3BH

Stories first published 1981 under the title
Bible Stories for Today. The Old Testament

This edition first published 1992
Reprinted 1993

ISBN 0 900274-53-0

Acknowledgement
The poem on page 210 is reproduced by kind permission of
Oxford University Press from *The Winding Quest*, by Alan Dale.

Designed by Topics Visual Information, Exeter

Cover photograph by Jamie Simson

Illustrations by Topics Visual Information

Typeset by ICON, Exeter

Printed in Great Britain by BPCC Wheatons Ltd, Exeter
for Chansitor Publications Ltd, Norwich

Preface
to
First Edition

In attempting to retell these Bible stories I have been conscious of trying to do four things.

First, I have tried to write for children. In so doing I hope I have avoided childish writing. The Bible is not childish. Its children grew up quickly in a world which was often harsh and uncompromising. Insipid characters were rare and reviled. Drama, excitement and danger were never far away.

Secondly, I have tried to be honest. The Bible narrative is based on history. That does not mean that all its stories are historical stories. There are stories of inner struggles as well as outer ones. Religiously speaking the former are more important than the latter. In my experience this seems to worry adults more than children, for whom the inner world is often very real.

Thirdly, I have tried not to moralize or sermonize. A good story tells itself, although sometimes its original context needs explanation. Experience has caused me to reject the belief that children should not be given these stories until they can understand them. Great stories, like great music, poetry and art, are never fully understood. Rather, we go on unpacking layer after layer of meaning as the years go by. Interpretation goes on at a variety of levels. At the heart of all religion lies a mystery.

Finally, I have tried to keep a balance over the whole of the Bible literature. Harsh selection has been unavoidable, but I have given priority to those stories which contribute to the development of The Story. The Bible is a unified collection of religious experiences. That is the wonder of it. Against those experiences we can measure our own and grow accordingly. That, I believe, is why we have a duty to go on telling these stories. That is why our children have a right to hear them.

J.G.P.

For
Matthew Brault and his generation

Contents

Note: Where a new title has been given to an already familiar story the traditional title is given in brackets.

Introduction
Story, Truth and Bible

STORY AND STORIES

'Read the Bible like any other book,' said the poet Samuel Taylor Coleridge, 'and you will quickly discover it is not like any other book you have ever read.'

This is exactly what we do not seem to be capable of doing any more, particularly in schools. Many teachers appear extremely uncomfortable with the Bible. They give all sorts of reasons which often appear more defensive than rational and frequently contradict one another. For example, many say that they cannot teach Bible stories because they do not believe them but they become confused very quickly when asked just what that means. To make matters even more complex the same teachers will very often be found using stories from other religious traditions, for example, from Hindu mythology, apparently with no qualms, even when they do not regard themselves as belonging to those faiths either.

Others will argue that it is not possible to gain the same enjoyment from Bible stories as from other literature because they are somehow 'special' or 'holy'. In other words interpretations are prescribed beforehand and consequently both children and teachers are inhibited from giving free rein to their own imaginations. Again these teachers are often at pains to point out that they do not regard themselves as believers. It is usually someone else's tradition they are safeguarding. In the main this group are what we might term alienated Christians. Jews, to whom the bulk of this material belongs and who were responsible for the writing of all but a tiny fraction of it, seem to have far less of a problem. By and large they can relax in it, enjoy it, laugh with it in places, argue with it in others and generally treat it as a normal and indispensable part of any education which is concerned with passing on the culture.

There is a third group which simply says that this material is old fashioned, out of date and boring. They argue that neither teachers nor children see the point in telling Bible stories any more. There are simply more important things to fill up curriculum time with. In its own way this attitude is as confessional as its opposite, based as it is on minds already convinced that their evaluation is final and not subject to challenge or change. To this group there is only one answer and it is the Coleridgean one – give the Bible a chance, try it and see. These stories must survive on their own merit but honesty must surely serve to make us recognize that they have already survived longer than most and that perhaps there are reasons for that, contained within the stories themselves. It has to be said that the argument of this group is more persuasive when it is based on knowledge of what is being rejected.

The first two arguments are more subtle because they involve issues other than straight reasoning. There is confusion, there is often a sense of guilt and there is, most of all, an awareness of deep ignorance. Coleridge was fortunate. He was involved right at the beginning of the whole opening up of the Bible to scientific criticism. In his time he probably understood what was starting to happen, especially in Germany, better than any other person in Britain and it did not worry him. He was a poet and he knew a great deal about the nature of poetry and how poets, as distinct from scientists, went about searching for and expressing truth. However, when he advised us to read the Bible like any other book it was not a scientific textbook or even necessarily a history book he had in mind. Read the Bible, he was saying, just like any other book of stories and then find out for yourself whether it is just like any other story-book. It seems a fair test.

In terms of school knowledge the question is one of entitlement. Rabbi Lionel Blue in one of his 'Thought for the Day' broadcasts on BBC Radio 4 illustrated this perfectly when he pin-pointed the familiar issue of telling stories which we may or may not believe in, but gave it an unexpected twist. He cited a Jewish woman who was held by some of her friends to be something of a hypocrite because she claimed not to have any religious beliefs but, nevertheless, in her own words, 'kept the observances' for her children. Her reply to her accusers was simple. 'What right have I to break the tradition? Maybe they will want to become believers even if I don't.'

The school's job is primarily to inform. Quite apart from any questions of personal belief and faith, not to know these stories is to break with tradition, to cut a future generation off from much which has permeated the past and to leave it ignorant and alienated from much of its history, its literature, its music, its art and architecture and the general rhythm of its life, which is the legacy of its traditional religion and even of its attitude towards other faiths. The languages of Europe retain thousands of biblical images, even if many of them seem to be used mainly as profanities. Every city, town and village possesses its church. Less discernible but most persistent of all, many of our moral and cultural attitudes come out of the biblical experience whether we like it or not. The 'hidden curriculum' is a relatively modern invention of a society which perhaps would rather not know where its values come from.

At the same time those who do not know where they stand have problems in moving forward. The stories in this book are some of the very earliest expressions of the values of Western civilization. That is why our children are entitled to know them and to explore them. Professionally speaking the individual teacher's personal beliefs about the Bible are of no more significance than their personal opinions about Roundheads and Cavaliers, but then that too is a piece of English history impossible to teach adequately to pupils with no knowledge of the Bible.

Coleridge's first suggestion then was that we should simply try to tell Bible stories like any other story. His second point, however, is that when we do so we are likely to find that they are in some sense different. The important thing is to realize that the educational discovery has to be that way round. If what he says is true then children will discover it **for themselves**. If it is not true then that is the end of it for that particular child. What is not acceptable is for children to be told beforehand that these stories are different so that they are never fully attended to as story because other considerations get in the way. The child must always be free to gather insights which the teacher may lack. For what Coleridge is saying is distinctive about these stories is not that they are made special or in some way sanctified by any external body but that the material itself simply goes deeper than other literature.

There are, very broadly speaking, three categories of story. There is, first, the ephemeral 'soap opera' type which merely reflects, and thereby reinforces, social mores. Its primary function is to entertain and it rarely does more than that as it fills our television screens, magazines and many books.

Secondly, there is that to which we attribute the title 'literature'. Literature endures. It possesses a depth which goes beyond the circumstances of the story itself, and the term covers a whole range from Shakespeare to folk-tales. It holds a mirror up to life, points to something basic in the human condition and, in doing so, confronts us ourselves. Literature has to do with ethics (ideals) as much as with mores (how we actually behave) and, for that reason, has an important part to play in moral education in its own right. We teach literature because children are entitled to be aware of the highest and the best that humankind has conceived, as well as of what humanity is really like.

There is then a third category, to which we give the name 'myth'. It does not help that our contemporary use of language has distorted that word to the point where it has become counterproductive to use it. Just as story-telling has become synonymous with lying so a myth is generally seen as something which is untrue, a classic example of what Wittgenstein called the 'bewitchment of language'.

Perhaps we need to start again and simply resort to using the original Greek word *mythos* if only because the term is vacuous and not soiled by prejudice from the start. *Mythos* represents the deepest story form of all. It comes nearer to poetry than anything else, which is perhaps why poets recognize its value more quickly than the rest of us. If we search for a modern analogy then the seemingly unlikely image of the warhead of a cruise missile is not inappropriate. We are told that it is very small, not much larger than a cricket ball, but when released it has the power to devastate whole cities and to radiate out even further. So it is, only in a constructive way, with myths or *mythoi*. In appearance they are simple and innocent little stories but they contain a highly compressed mass which, when released, influences whole civilizations, feeds whole literatures and endures not just down the centuries but down the millennia.

Thus Ted Hughes, the Poet Laureate and writer of children's fiction, can talk, in an essay entitled 'Myth and Education', of the religious myth as 'irreducible, a lump of the world', which 'can never be diminished by the seemingly infinite mass of theological agonising … which has attempted to translate it into something more manageable'. Hughes, it should be said, has never laid claim to 'being religious'.

What matters in teaching these stories is simply that children should know and enjoy them. It is Ted Hughes again who talks of children 'entering and leaving such stories at will'. We do not have to tell children what they mean because there are layers upon layers of meaning and none of us is able, with absolute certainty, to say that we have the final, conclusive meaning. The stories must be left open and not closed off from future exploration. But we cannot enter into them and explore them at all unless we are told them in the first place.

So much, then, for story but we have still left the vexed question of truth untouched.

TRUTH AND TRUTHS

If truth remains the problem then it is a problem which is vested not so much in these stories as in ourselves. Pontius Pilate's question 'What is truth?' continues to reverberate down the centuries but it is unlikely that there was ever a time when the question was more urgent than it is now. It is education's task to open children's eyes to the various ways in which truth is communicated but we in the West in general, and in Britain in particular, are woefully unskilled these days in the use of any form of truth criteria other than those of mathematics and science.

Philosophers are acutely aware of our difficulties but my own awareness of the depth of the problem came to me in a personal encounter some years ago. It was the hyena story which brought it about.

I was teaching at the time in a primary teacher training college in a remote part of rural Zambia. Our students came from two contrasting areas. Those from the north had been educated in village schools out in the bush and were steeped in the culture of Africa. The others came from the towns of the Copperbelt, with its Europeanized culture and its Western-style schools.

The hyena story which, for reasons I can no longer recall, we were discussing that day came from the Nyanja people of Eastern Zambia and Malawi. It was a simple story of a hungry hyena vainly searching for food. It arrived, ravenous, at a fork in the path and hesitated about which way to go. It sniffed to the left and, in the far distance, at last smelt food. Beginning to move on, it hesitated, turned its head and sniffed to the right. Again, food. Which way should it go? The hunger pains became unbearable. It moved left and right, right and left undecided and indecisive, becoming more and more frantic in its movements like a demented disco dancer. In the end, with mounting frustration, it tried to go in both directions at once, tore itself in two and died!

Was the story true? The question, for some reason, was asked. Half of the group – the Copperbelt half it later transpired – immediately burst into laughter. Of course not! No one believed that old tribal rubbish any more. The others looked increasingly hurt. 'But it is true; it is true,' they began to mutter. The laughter only increased. 'Where do you think it happened?' they were asked. They were nonplussed and could not reply. 'When did it happen?' They were pressed and pressed on these points. Was there ever a time and place where all this occurred? No, but they would not give in, repeating again and again, 'It is true, it is true.' Further words of explanation failed them.

In the end it came with a rush. 'It is true. Greed kills.'

In recounting this it is not my intention to suggest that the biblical narrative is of the same literary form as this African folk-tale. I simply make the point that there are certain types of

4

truth which are better communicated by narrative than by proposition. The Bible contains many, many different types of account. The oversimplified question 'Is it true?' means something different in each case. Children have to be taught this differentiation.

The real problem is that many modern-day adults are themselves unsure of the various types of truth claims they are dealing with. This, I am convinced, is the main reason why so many primary teachers shy away from biblical material and make their excuses. It is perfectly acceptable to debate in what sense Orwell's *Animal Farm* or Swift's *Gulliver's Travels* (both written for adults and long used with children incidentally) may contain truth but when a Hebrew writer of the fourth century B.C.E. produces an exact literary parallel, which we have come to call the Book of Jonah, we are apt to go looking for whales in the Eastern Mediterranean and to be found arguing about how long a person could survive inside a fish as ways of ascertaining 'truth'!

There are straight historical accounts in this collection of stories (e.g. Story 24). There are other stories where the historical background is strong (e.g. Stories 28, 33, 38, 42) but in which there is more truth than just the straight historical facts. There are others which are outside history altogether. Adam and Eve did not exist, it is often said, but it might be truer to state that Adam and Eve have always existed. The Everyman tradition is strong in English literature. We should not be surprised that it – and the Everywoman tradition – is even stronger in Hebrew literature. What is the truth question? That the world began like that or that human beings are just like that?

The Zambian experience revealed my problem as a Westerner. I instinctively asked the question 'Is it true?' and not the much more important questions 'Does it convey truth?' or 'What does it mean?' Because we do not encourage children to ask these latter questions they can grow up missing vast areas of insight from both the past and the present. We pride ourselves on the 'knowledge explosion', the 'new knowledge', while throwing away the key which makes old knowledge still available to us. (See Addendum, p. 8.)

The question 'Is it true?' is the basic question of a scientific culture. It assumes exactness, literalism and some form of empirical verification. By contrast the question 'Does it contain truth?' belongs to the world of the arts, to the theatre audience, the concert goer and the literary critic. No exactness is looked for; a degree of subjectivity is assumed because it is recognized that the artist, in whatever form, is attempting to express and draw our attention to an inner experience which it is beyond the possibility of literal words to express. For some strange inexplicable reason we seem unable to treat any material which bears the label 'religious' in the same way even though such material is the basic inspiration of the vast majority of our art, drama, music and literature.

The philosopher Ludwig Wittgenstein catches this point exactly and very simply when he says, 'People nowadays think that scientists exist to instruct them, poets, musicians etc. to give them pleasure. The idea that these have something to teach them – that does not occur to them.' (*Culture and Value*, p. 36)

in another passage in the same book he turns to the Bible story as an example of something which is not 'just a story' but is not 'just history' either. Talking specifically of the Christian gospels he remarks on the fact that there are four different accounts and judges this to be a good thing simply because history is not the sole or perhaps even the most important truth test with this material.

5

It is important that this narrative should not be more than quite averagely historically plausible **just so that** this should not be taken as the essential, decisive thing, so that the **letter** should not be believed more strongly than is proper and the **spirit** may receive its due, i.e. what you are supposed to see cannot be communicated even by the best and most accurate historian; and, therefore, a mediocre account suffices, is even to be preferred. For that too can tell you what you are supposed to be told, roughly in the way a mediocre stage set can be better than a sophisticated one, painted trees better than real ones, − because these might distract attention from what matters.

(*Culture and Value*, p. 31)

Adults who very freely comment on whether they 'believe in it or not' might do well to ponder these words very carefully before passing on their own certainties to children. For the one outstanding characteristic of this material is that no one has total mastery of it. It is all too easy to tell others what the story means but that is to overlook the fact that there may be layers of meaning, some of which may be seen by the teacher but some of which may not. The one great fact about religious education, which distinguishes it from other subjects, is that a young child may well have insights denied even to a university professor!

BIBLE AND BOOKS

It was as long ago as 1964 that Ronald Goldman, at the conclusion of a long piece of research, declared that 'the Bible is not a children's book'. This statement had a devastating effect on the use of this material. Had he declared at the time that there was far too much of it in most syllabuses then few, if any, would have questioned his judgement. As it is it now has to be said that in his declaration he was simply wrong. There is no other part of the world in which the basic, traditional religious stories of any culture are denied to children on the grounds that they cannot be fully understood. Nobody of whatever age or intelligence has ever fully understood them. They are not that sort of material. The Bible is not a historical textbook, although it contains a lot of history. It is, first and foremost, a library, a collection of different sorts of writings compiled over a long period of time, well over a thousand years.

What the Bible really is is a collection of religious experiences and spiritual insights. All the great, enduring questions of human existence are here, including major dreams and visions for a better world. These can only be told, as it were, from the inside.

All the great religions of the world have begun in the context of one person alone, whether it was Abraham under the stars, Moses at the burning bush, Gautama Buddha under the tree, Jesus in the wilderness (or on the Cross) or the Prophet Muhammad in the cave. Inward experience can be communicated only via the medium of imagery. Often this is non-verbal and takes the form of music, dance or visual art. When language is used it is the language of metaphor and simile. There is poetry and parable, there are personal letters and public pronouncements; occasionally there is only silence (e.g. Story 31). Above all there is, for us, the need to know the difference. To reduce all this to mere learning of externals is to shatter vision, to destroy dreams and to reduce the inspiration of our forebears into the pathetically mundane.

6

A whole generation has now grown up since the Goldman research more or less imposed a ban on the use of the Bible in school. One result has been a generation of teachers who themselves find this material strange and bewildering. This collection was originally produced as one person's response to the Goldman fallacy. It has proved popular in many schools but it was quickly realized that many teachers needed something more by way of background. This revision has tried to meet that need in as simple a way as possible, bearing in mind that teachers nowadays have little time to read and none at all to study new areas in any depth.

HOW TO USE THIS BOOK

The stories are presented as before to be read to or by children either in the classroom or in assembly. In addition, however, we have now added two Notes sections to each story.

At the end of each telling there is a section entitled 'About the Story'. These short passages attempt to explain why the story has been written in the way it has, where it fits into the whole Bible narrative and to give other background information. The aim is simply to allow the teacher some degree of confidence in telling the story. **These sections are not intended for study by children**.

There follows a section entitled 'Ideas for Exploring Further'. They are just that. They are not intended as a substitute for any teacher's own original ideas and they are in no way intended to be regarded as exhaustive. What Angela Horton has attempted to do is to put forward ideas which add a genuinely religious dimension of thinking to integrated topic work as opposed to turning the religious-education component back into something indistinguishable from historical or geographical input. She has also, wherever appropriate, linked up the stories to named study units and/or attainment targets within the National Curriculum, showing how religious-education work can be accommodated with integrity in mainstream work thus helping to ensure some economy of that most precious classroom commodity – time.

Abbreviations   References to areas of the National Curriculum are preceded by the symbol ■. The abbreviations AT, CSU and SSU stand for 'attainment target', 'core (History) study unit' and 'supplementary (History) study unit', respectively.

CONCLUSION

The Education Reform Act of 1988 gives little choice in the matter of whether or not the Bible is any longer taught. It forms a compulsory part of all Agreed Syllabuses of Religious Education. What is essential is that it should be treated within the traditions of the best imaginative educational practice and without anxiety on the part of teachers who, quite rightly, even if sometimes a little unreflectively, do not want to be seen in the role of propagating religious beliefs. All that is asked is that these stories be seen as important enough to warrant diligent attention in the primary curriculum and, in view of their place in our heritage, it would be hard to deny that request.

The crucial question is **how** they are presented. Maria Harris, an American teacher, sums up much of our argument very concisely when she says:

Religious education must be related to the search for truth. Such truth, however, is not so much the truth of fact, where the opposite of a true statement is a false statement, or even where some things are false and others true. It is rather the truth of art, where some things are adequate and others are more adequate.

As in the teaching of art, these stories will do their own work, or not, and that work is quite unpredictable. What is required of us professionally is that we do not deny the possibility to future generations.

Jack Priestley
Christmas 1991

AN ADDENDUM TO THE HYENA STORY

What I was privileged to observe happening in a very short space of time in an African setting has, of course, happened in Europe over a much longer period of time. One has only to look at the entry for 'story' in the full *Oxford English Dictionary* or in any good etymological dictionary to see this.

All of the earliest examples denote a form of communication which is directly related to truth. A story is a 'narrative true or supposed to be true'. It is 'the same as history, a branch of knowledge as opposed to fiction'. However, as we move into the eighteenth century and beyond, the definitions become more and more hedged about with qualifications. A story becomes 'a recital of events alleged to have happened'. It is 'a narrative of real, or more usually fictitious events', 'a particular person's representation of a matter', until finally we reach a point where the word 'story', once synonymous with truth, is now deemed to convey the exact opposite. The last dictionary entry, from our own century, is 'a colloquialism for a lie, as in the phrase "you story-teller"'.

It is as if the whole history of Western thought since the Middle Ages has been compressed and is contained within this one dictionary definition. What has changed is not the form of story so much as our concept of what constitutes truth. Our culture has undergone a change to the point that we are becoming cut off from the past, unable to penetrate its thought patterns. There are certain questions we no longer even ask or train our children to ask. This is at root our fundamental problem in teaching from all ancient texts. The Bible is no exception.

8

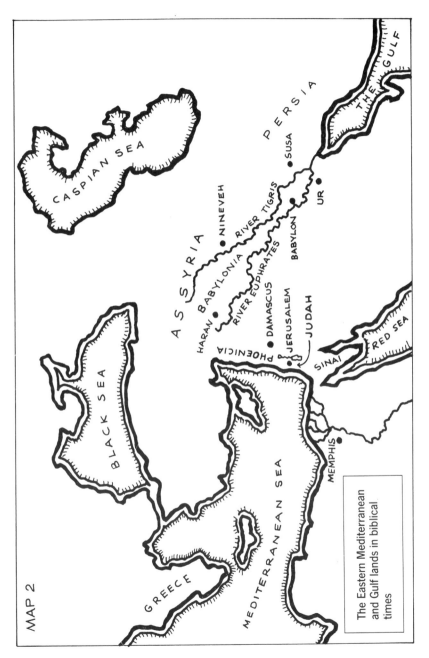

MAP 2

CASPIAN SEA

THE GULF

PERSIA

SUSA

ASSYRIA

NINEVEH

RIVER TIGRIS

UR

BABYLONIA

HARAN

BABYLON

RIVER EUPHRATES

DAMASCUS

JERUSALEM

JUDAH

PHOENICIA

RED SEA

SINAI

BLACK SEA

MEMPHIS

MEDITERRANEAN SEA

GREECE

The Eastern Mediterranean
and Gulf lands in biblical
times

9

1
Get Up and Go

Genesis 12: 1 – 13: 18

It all began with Abraham. And it started in the city of Haran.
Haran was a pleasant town. It stood near the banks of the great
Euphrates river. Its streets were lined with palm trees. Many
of the people who lived there were rich. Their houses were
large and stood in beautiful gardens.

Haran was a busy town. It stood on the desert road which
came from the East. Merchants, with their camels, brought
silks and spices from China. They travelled on to the West – to
the cities of Europe and Africa. The market at Haran was
always full of colour and life. All around was the desert, dry
and bare. Haran was a good place to live.

Abraham should have been happy and contented. He
wasn't. He was restless. Deep down inside him he kept hear-
ing a voice. Over and over again it kept saying, 'Abraham, get
up. Pack your things. Leave your house. Say goodbye to all
your friends. Go out into the desert. Leave the city behind
you.' Abraham knew it was the voice of God.

Abraham did not want to move. He liked living in Haran.
He was getting old. He tried to shut out the voice. He
couldn't. It came again and again. 'Abraham,' it would say,
'go where I show you. You will become the father of a great
nation. Get up and go.'

But where? thought Abraham. If only I knew where to go.
The desert is endless. It is hot and dry. People get lost in it.
They wander for weeks and die. I'm too old to move.

'Go,' said the voice inside him again. 'Have faith. Believe in me. Then you will be remembered for ever.'

Abraham went. He packed all his things on to mules and camels. He took his wife Sarah and all his servants. All his sheep and his goats walked with him. He took his nephew as well. His nephew's name was Lot.

They left the wide streets of Haran and walked to the west, towards the setting sun. Day after day, week after week, they walked. The days were very hot; the nights were very cold. They turned from the west and moved to the south. The desert seemed to have no end.

Abraham felt very tired. Where would it end? Why had he listened to this strange voice inside him? Why had he left Haran? He must be very stupid. At night he lay awake. Should he turn back?

Suddenly he heard the voice again. 'Get up,' it said. 'Go outside.' Abraham threw off his goatskin blanket. He went outside the tent. 'Look up,' said the voice. 'Count the stars.'

Abraham looked upwards. It was a clear night. The stars covered the sky. 'I can't count all those,' said Abraham. 'There must be millions of them.'

'Your descendants will be like that,' said the voice. 'There will be millions of them. You are going to be the father of a great people. Go on. I will lead you.'

Abraham moved on. For many more days they walked south. Then one day they came to a place which was very bare and rocky. Suddenly, Abraham knew he had to stop. He looked around. There was hardly any grass at all. Could this really be the place? They put up their tents.

A few days later a servant came to Abraham's tent. 'Come quickly,' said the servant. 'The herdsmen are fighting.'

Abraham ran outside. His nephew Lot was there as well. 'What's going on?' asked Abraham.

'There is not enough grass for our sheep and Lot's sheep,' came the reply. 'Your shepherds and his started to argue about it. Then they started to fight.'

'This won't do,' Abraham said to Lot. 'We must split up.'

11

Abraham was the elder. He could have chosen where to go, but he let Lot choose instead. Lot looked around. Far, far away to the east he could see trees. There must be water there. 'I'll go that way,' said Lot.

'In that case,' replied Abraham, 'I will move to the west.' They said goodbye to one another.

Abraham and his family moved on. Suddenly he heard the voice again. 'Look around you,' it said. They were on high ground. Abraham could see for miles. 'Look north and south, east and west,' said the voice. 'This land is for you and your descendants. Stop here.'

Abraham was in the land of Canaan. He pitched his tent for the last time near some oak trees. Nearby was a place called Hebron. He would build a city there. One day it would be the centre of a nation. It was what the voice of God had told him to do.

NOTES

ABOUT THE STORY

Why start with Abraham? It is something of an arbitrary choice. We could start elsewhere. In terms of the full Bible as story it would be right to start with Creation (see Stories 46, 47). If we wanted to start with documented history we might begin somewhere between the Moses stories and the accounts of King David. Abraham, however, is the father figure of the Jewish people and, although written up much later than the actual events, this story is regarded by them as marking their origins.

These first stories (Stories 1–10) of the early Patriarchs, or the male founders of the Jewish people, are shrouded in the mists of time. They need to be told with an air of mystery and uncertainty – a stepping-out into the unknown. There can be little doubt that in this period, about four thousand years ago, there were significant migrations around the Fertile Crescent formed by the Tigris and Euphrates rivers, between Ur and Haran (see map on p.9) – the journey reputed to have been made by Abraham's father. This story recounts the move onwards out of relative security into the unknown wastelands, which in time were to become the Promised Land of Israel.

Historical and geographical exactness, however, is not what this story is about. Like most of the stories which follow it is told, as it were, from the inside. It is to do with the qualities required to have faith in an inner conviction and to act.

It may be worthwhile to note that Abraham is a figure much revered in Islam as well as amongst Jews and Christians.

IDEAS FOR EXPLORING FURTHER

Migration   Use maps to indicate places where children have lived. Discuss reasons why people move. Is it an easy decision to make? What would we feel like if we had to move next week? Make a picture of a large pair of scales on which to place ideas for and against moving. Compare with ideas Abraham may have had and emphasize the complexity of decision-making. Discuss people in the news who are moving and the reasons. Collect newspaper/magazine pictures. Make speech/thought bubbles to accompany each picture to show reasons for migration, hopes and fears, responsibilities towards other people, conflicting emotions about staying/leaving. How important is it to welcome new people into the community? (Cf. *Refugees*, by Linda Wilcox.)

Places and Values   Ask what makes a 'good', 'bad' or 'special' place. How do pupils feel about such places? Invite people of different religious traditions to explain what they feel about their places of worship. Ask children what they value most in their locality/region/country. Discuss how people alter their environment. What could be suggested for improving the environment? Design and make a special environment and say what is particularly valued in it. (**NC** *Geography*: ATs 2, 4, 5; *Technology*: designing and making an environment) How have people valued places in the past? (**NC** *History*: CSU 3 – Victorian Britain; CSU 6 – exploration and encounters 1450–1550)

2

Give All You Have

Genesis 22: 1–14

Abraham and Sarah had a son. They called him Isaac. It was a funny name. It meant 'laughter'. When he had been born they were so happy that they laughed and laughed. That was why they had given him the name. He was their only child. One day he would take over from Abraham.

Then one day the voice came to Abraham again. It stopped him laughing. 'Give me the most precious thing you've got,' it said. 'Show how strong your faith really is.'

Abraham thought. He knew what the answer was. Isaac was his most precious possession. How could he give up his son? It was the custom to offer things to God by making sacrifices. That meant killing something and then burning it. Could Abraham kill Isaac? He knew that if he did he would never laugh again. But it seemed as if he would have to.

Next morning Abraham got up early. He woke Isaac and said, 'Get up. We are going on a journey. We are going to make a sacrifice to God.'

'Where?' asked Isaac, jumping up from his bed.

'In the mountains,' was all Abraham would say.

They set off with donkeys and two servants. One of the donkeys carried wood for the fire. The others carried food for the journey. They walked up into the hills. On the third day Abraham stopped. In front of them was a steep hill, almost a mountain.

14

'Wait here,' Abraham said to the servants. 'The boy and I will go up the hill alone. Unload the donkey.'

The servants took the wood off the donkey's back. Isaac had to carry it. He was bent double under the weight but he was very strong. Abraham lit a fire. With it he set light to a torch. He carried it in one hand. He would need the flame to start a fire up on the mountain. In the other hand he carried a large knife. They set off. Isaac stopped.

'Father,' he said, 'haven't we forgotten something?'

Abraham said nothing. He pretended not to hear. Isaac went on.

'We've got the wood, the fire and the knife. But what are we going to sacrifice? Shouldn't we have an animal?'

Abraham paused. This was the moment he had been frightened of. 'Don't worry,' he said at last, 'God will provide something when we get there.'

He walked on. Isaac followed, carrying his heavy load. Slowly they made their way to the very top of the hill. At the top they stopped. Isaac put down the wood. Together he and Abraham collected some large stones. They built an altar. It was like a large table. The work was hard. Isaac was very tired. He sat down.

Suddenly Abraham seized hold of Isaac. He tied his hands and feet with a piece of rope he had kept hidden under his cloak. Then he lifted Isaac up and put him, face down, on the stone altar. Abraham reached for his knife. He must do it quickly. He raised the knife high. He took a deep breath and. . . .

His arm would not move. It was as if something were holding it above his head. The voice came to him again. 'Abraham, Abraham,' it called urgently.

Abraham looked upwards. There was nothing there except the blue sky.

'Don't touch your son. Don't harm him,' called the voice. 'Let Isaac go free. That is not the sort of sacrifice I want.'

Abraham felt his arm go loose. He lowered his hand and dropped the knife. Quickly he untied Isaac. When Abraham looked round he noticed something he had not seen before. There was a ram caught in a bush. Abraham and Isaac wanted to make some sacrifice to God. They killed the ram. It was the custom. But never again would they kill a human being. The God of Abraham did not want that.

When they reached the bottom of the hill Abraham looked back. 'It is a holy place,' he said. 'It must have a name. I shall call it "The Lord Shall Provide".' He did not know that one day a city would be built on the hill. Its name was to be 'Jerusalem'.

NOTES

ABOUT THE STORY

We come immediately to one of the most difficult stories in the whole Bible and yet one it is hard to omit. No single explanation can be offered. It seems to represent an impossible and totally illogical situation. Abraham has been called to become the father of a great nation but to sacrifice his only son is the one act which would destroy any possibility of that ever happening.

Within that contradiction lies perhaps the deepest religious value of this story. It is possible for inner convictions to be no more than self-interest, piously expressed. Abraham is caught in the dilemma of whether or not he really trusts in God totally and completely.

Explicit in this story too is the rejection of the idea of human sacrifice within the religion of the Hebrews, in marked contrast with other groups around them at this period.

However, there are other motifs present, about which we really know very little. Excavations at Ur have revealed carvings of rams caught in a thicket, at the entrance to graveyards. Mystery and uncertainty, conviction accompanied by nagging doubt are all elements within this account.

Decisiveness cannot always depend on rational proof. And what about Sarah? In telling this story one might imagine that she would have had some feelings on the subject!

IDEAS FOR EXPLORING FURTHER

Action, Not Talk Discuss how sacred writings ask people to put God's work and other people's interests first. Draw out the need for action, not just talk, for helping people, sharing belongings, acting responsibly, giving to charity. Work in groups to make a chart showing what this would mean in the classroom or home.

Trust Talk with younger pupils about what we trust children, parents, teachers, friends, doctors to do, and what people feel when let down. Make life-size smiling or sad people carrying banners (saying, e.g., 'I feel let down when my brother/sister breaks the toys I lend', 'I trust my mum to give me food', 'I know my doctor will try to make me well', 'I can trust my friend not to tell tales about me'). Ask older children how trust operates in the world around them. For example, at a supermarket, we trust the door to be open; goods to be on the shelves, labelled and priced; a person to be at the check-out with a till that functions; bags to be available. What if this were not so? What about the trust we put in hospitals, firemen, banks? What if people betrayed the trust put in them to do a job properly and just did as they liked? What is the role of free will in all this? Plenty of scope for stories and poems and writing a scene to reflect these issues! (NC *English*) See also notes on Story 50.

Sacrifice Draw or describe a highly desired object or event. What would we give/ sacrifice for it? Compare ideas. Is 'sacrifice' meaningful only if it is 'painful'? (NC *History*: CSU 4 – Second World War, e.g. the people who sheltered Anne Frank or Douglas Bader; inventors sacrificing leisure time)

17

3

The Story of Rebekah

Genesis 24

Isaac had grown up. Who could he marry? Abraham wanted him to have a wife from his own people. He did not want him to marry a woman from Canaan. He would have to go back to the city of Haran. Abraham was too old to go. He was worried. Suppose Isaac went to Haran. Would he ever come back?

Abraham sent for Eliezer. Eliezer was his most trusted servant.

'I have a job for you,' said Abraham. 'It is a very special job.'

'You know I will do anything for you,' replied Eliezer.

'Go to Haran. Find there a girl who will make a good wife for Isaac. Bring her back here.'

Eliezer was worried. 'Suppose she won't come?' he asked. 'After all, Haran is a beautiful town. They will not know Canaan and they will not know Isaac either. Let me take him with me.'

'No,' said Abraham. He spoke very firmly. 'Isaac must never go back to Haran. God led me to this place. Here we must stay. This is where our children and grandchildren must grow into a great people. Go to Haran alone. Do what you can. If you fail, come back. I am very old. I may not live until you return. But promise me that if I am dead you will never show Isaac the way back to Haran.'

Eliezer promised. He took ten camels and loaded them with gifts. Then he set off across the desert. It was a long, long journey. All the time he kept thinking how he could do the job which Abraham had given him.

At last the walls of Haran came into sight. The camels moved forward more quickly. They could smell water. The well was outside the city walls. The women came there every day to collect water. They were there now.

The camels stopped. Eliezer got down. As he did so he was still saying the prayer he had been muttering for days.

'O God, help me to find the right wife for Isaac.'

He looked up. The women were pulling their full buckets out of the well. It was hard work in the hot sun. Suddenly he had an idea. This was a good place to find a generous woman. He moved over towards the well. Some of the women saw him coming. They put their water jars on their heads and walked away.

Eliezer sat down and waited. Another woman came towards the well. She was young. Eliezer noticed that she was also very attractive. The woman let down the bucket. That was easy. Then she had to pull the full bucket to the top again. That was hard work. Finally she poured the water into her jar. She was about to put it on her head when Eliezer spoke to her.

'Could I have a drop of your water, please?' he asked. 'I have come on a long journey. I am very tired.'

'Of course,' said the girl, whose name was Rebekah. 'Drink as much as you like.'

Eliezer took the jar.

'Are those your ten camels?' asked Rebekah.

'Yes,' replied Eliezer.

'While you drink and rest I will give them water for you,' she said.

Rebekah turned back to the well. Again and again she lowered the bucket. Again and again she heaved it to the top. She poured the water into a trough. The camels were very thirsty. They drank a lot of water.

Eliezer watched. This is the woman for Isaac, he thought. But how can I make her come with me?

He went over to his camel. From the saddle-bag he took a

19

gold ring and two bracelets. He gave them to Rebekah. 'Take these,' he said. 'Go to your father. Tell him I should like to talk to him. Perhaps he has a room where I could stay for the night.'

'We have a room and we have straw for the camels,' Rebekah replied. 'Wait here.' She ran off.

A few minutes later a man came out of the city gates. It was Laban, Rebekah's brother. He helped Eliezer lead the camels to the house. The father of Laban and Rebekah was called Bethuel. Before they even had time for a meal Eliezer told Bethuel and Laban why he had come.

Next morning Laban spoke to Rebekah. He told her what Eliezer wanted. 'Will you go with this man?' he asked. 'Will you marry Isaac the son of Abraham who left this town many years ago?'

'I will go,' said Rebekah, 'I also believe in God's call. This has been planned by him. I will make the journey to an unknown land. I will marry this man I do not know.'

Eliezer left many gifts with Laban and Bethuel. With Rebekah behind him he set off on the long journey home. It had been easier than he could ever have dreamed.

When they got back to Canaan Abraham was still there. Isaac and Rebekah were married. Their first children were twins, two brothers. They called them Esau and Jacob.

ABOUT THE STORY

Traditionally these early biblical figures have been known as the Patriarchs. It might be better to use the word 'Founders'. In this desert society women have always been portrayed as very subordinate to men. And yet it is also the case that the few women who come to the fore within the narrative are strong minded and independent. We have to remember that the history has been written largely by men and also that we ourselves are only slowly emerging from a period of patriarchal dominance.

In the general tone of this story there is much which is immediately recognizable to those whose ethnic origins lie in Africa or Asia. Nor is it very far removed from the experience of Caucasian Europeans. There is desire for marriage within the group or clan. Like millions of migrants down the ages Abraham sends 'home' for a spouse for his child. The marriage is arranged; the couple do not meet beforehand.

At the same time it is worth noting that even in this ancient period the qualities being looked for are those of character rather than mere physical beauty and attraction. Rebekah is no passive agent in the proceedings. In her society, as in most others until very recent times, there was simply no place for the single woman, but she is not treated merely as a piece of property. Her own personality is a key factor in this and in the following story.

IDEAS FOR EXPLORING FURTHER

Choosing a Friend or Partner   Ask pupils to design an advertisement requesting a friend or a partner for themselves or someone they like very much. Raise issues concerning significant personal qualities, the importance of not judging people by appearances, and the value of actions which speak louder than words. Discuss with older children the need for common interests, loyalty, trust, responsibility, flexibility, perseverance, a sense of humour.

Marriage Customs   Talk about marriages children have attended and what happens at a wedding service. Does a marriage join together two individuals or two families? Use art work to reflect different religious/national customs and compare. (NC *Geography*: AT 2 – knowledge and understanding of places) See also Story 40.

Gender Roles within the Community   Ask older pupils to reconstruct Rebekah's role within her home and community. Examine gender roles at different periods. (NC *History*: all HSUs and local study) Devise a questionnaire to ask great-grandparents, grandparents and others about employment opportunities open to them, toys used, clothes worn, etc. Use the data to construct graphs/pie-charts. (NC *Mathematics*: using and applying mathematics; *Information Technology*) Compare past and present employment opportunities. (NC *Careers Education*) Compare opportunities in Britain with other localities. (NC *Geography*: AT 2)

4

A Quarrel between Two Brothers

Genesis 25: 27–34; 27: 1–45

Esau and Jacob were twins, but they were not at all alike. Esau was big and strong. He loved to hunt. He was his father's favourite. Jacob was quiet and clever. He liked to stay at home. He was his mother's favourite. The two boys did not like each other at all. They were always fighting and quarrelling.

One day Esau came back from a long hunting trip. He had caught nothing. Half dead with hunger he staggered home. Jacob was cooking. Esau could smell it before he reached the house. He was so hungry it nearly drove him mad.

'Give me some of that,' he gasped, stretching out his hand for the pan.

'Not so fast,' said Jacob, snatching the pan away. 'What's it worth?'

'Come on, let me have it,' begged Esau. 'I haven't eaten for days.'

He tried to grab the pan again. Jacob once more stepped out of the way.

'What's it worth?' he asked for the second time.

'Anything you like,' groaned Esau.

'Right,' replied Jacob. 'You were born just before me. So you are the elder son. You get all the privileges. Hand them over to me. Give me your birthright. Let me be treated as the elder brother.'

'Done,' said Esau without thinking. 'I can't eat a birthright and I'm starving. If I don't eat soon I shall die.'

Jacob made Esau swear solemnly. Then he gave him some food. Afterwards Esau was angry. But there was nothing he could do about it.

A few years later Jacob did the same thing again.

Isaac was getting old. He was nearly blind. He knew he could not live much longer. He sent for Esau.

'I want to give you my blessing,' he said. 'But first, go out hunting. Make my favourite meat meal and bring it here.'

Esau went. As soon as he had gone Rebekah ran to find Jacob.

'Quickly,' she said, 'your father is going to give Esau his blessing. You must get it for yourself. Kill two goats. I will cook the meat so that it tastes like his favourite tasty dish. Then you must go and pretend you are Esau.'

'It won't work,' replied Jacob. 'Esau has got hairy skin. Mine is smooth. If my father touches me he will know who I am. Then I shall get a curse, not a blessing.'

'Let the curse come on me,' said Rebekah. 'Go and do as I say.'

She made the meal quickly. Then she took a piece of the goatskin and put it on the back of Jacob's hands. She got out Esau's best clothes and made Jacob put them on.

It worked.

'You've been quick,' said Isaac. 'Are you really Esau?'

'Yes, Father,' said Jacob. 'The hunting went well today.'

'Your voice sounds like Jacob's,' replied Isaac. He reached out and touched Jacob's hand. 'No,' he went on, 'I can tell you really are Esau. Your skin is covered in hair. Come here, my son.'

Jacob knelt down. Isaac put his hands on his head. He said, 'May God give you all the riches of the earth. You are to be the lord of everything round about. You will be the master over the family. They will serve you. Go now, my son.'

The old man was nearly crying. Jacob got up and ran from the room.

At that moment Esau came in. 'Here you are, Father,' he said cheerfully. 'I had some trouble hunting, but in the end I got what you wanted.'

Isaac knew the voice. He felt the hands. He knew he had been tricked. He trembled with rage. 'Your brother has tricked you,' he sobbed. 'He has stolen your blessing.'

'But Father,' said Esau, 'you must have one blessing left for me.'

'All I have for you is this,' whispered Isaac. 'You will live by fighting. Your brother must be your master, but in the end you will overcome him.'

Isaac died. Esau was in a fierce temper. 'When the funeral is over,' he shouted, 'I will kill my brother.'

Rebekah heard him. She ran to Jacob. 'Run,' she said, 'as fast as you can. Esau wants to murder you.'

'Where can I go?' asked Jacob.

'Go to Laban, your uncle. Stay there until I send for you. Run!'

Jacob ran from the house. He took only his staff. He hurried off into the desert alone.

ABOUT THE STORY

Unlike some other religions it is important to recognize that even the greatest hero figures of the Jews are never presented as perfect. That quality belongs to God alone. Jacob, who is to be renamed Israel, is flawed. He emerges from this account as the hero and victor but natural sympathies are with Esau.

This is one of those many stories which contain various layers of interpretation. How far the characters were genuine historical figures it is impossible to tell. Two aspects predominate. First, if Jacob is to become Israel, the father of the twelve tribes, then Esau is the progenitor and perhaps representative figure of their neighbours, the Edomites. Secondly, in an oral society oaths, blessings, cursings, etc., would be absolutely binding and an inheritance could not be divided.

The two brothers can perhaps also be seen as representative of contrasting qualities. Esau has right on his side. His virtues are the establishment virtues of loyalty, industry, patient time-serving and a somewhat unimaginative sense of duty. Jacob has to live by his wits, possessing no advantages other than the favouritism of his mother.

To later Jewish generations, deprived of land and resources through exile and dispersion, there is a real sense of identity with the outcome of this narrative but there is no great attempt at moral justification. It retains something of a simple 'brain over brawn' quality. Rebekah, too, the heroine of the previous story, may seem to be presented here as rather less than the perfect wife and mother but this incident must be judged in the light of what happens at the end of the Jacob narrative – see the next two stories.

IDEAS FOR EXPLORING FURTHER

Right or Wrong?   Discuss whether Jacob and Rebekah were right or wrong to do what they did. (Remember the values and social context of the deeds.) Draw out the mother's fears for her younger son, and that son's fears for his future because the inheritance could not be divided. Children may discover that it is all too easy to make hasty judgements about whether people's actions are right or wrong. Motives can be complex and it is important to try to understand them.

Actions Have Consequences   Think about how actions affect relationships. Imagine how Esau's and Isaac's relationship with Rebekah was affected by her deception. Ask older children to be reporters and to 'interview' Esau, Isaac, Rebekah, friends and servants after Jacob had fled. They could predict what will happen next. Alternatively, 'interview' Jacob five years after the event. What has happened to him since he left? Work on a script in small groups or ad lib. Older pupils can tape the interviews to make a 'radio programme' or write newspaper reports. (▨ *English*: ATs 1, 3; *Information Technology*) With younger pupils make a wall-sized cartoon to reflect their ideas.

5

Up to Heaven and Down to Earth

Genesis 28: 10–22; 29: 1–30

Jacob travelled north. He walked up into the hills. The ground was very stony. Nothing grew there.

The sun began to go down. Jacob was very tired. He had nowhere to go. He did not even have a tent. He would have to stop and sleep just where he was, among all the rocks. For a pillow he used a large stone. He lay down. Soon he was fast asleep.

As he slept he had a strange dream. It was very clear. The stone, which was his pillow, became a stair. Other stairs appeared above it. They went up and up as far as he could see. The top of the staircase disappeared into the sky.

Jacob saw something moving on the staircase. Some people were coming down the stairs. They were not ordinary people. They were angels. Down and down they came, one step at a time. When they reached the bottom stair they stepped on to the ground right through Jacob's head. Then he saw them going up again.

All through the night the angels went up and down the stairs. And every time they touched the ground they stepped through Jacob.

Suddenly Jacob woke up. He was shaking all over. He sat up and looked around. There was nothing there, just rocks and sand.

'This place frightens me,' said Jacob to himself. 'It is a holy place. It is the place where earth and heaven meet.'

Jacob stood up. He picked up the stone which he had used as a pillow. Then he carried it over to a pile of rocks. He stood it on its end on top of the pile. It looked like a monument. Jacob stood in front of it and made a vow. 'O God,' he said, 'if you will keep me safe on my journey I will make this a holy place for you. I call this place "Beth-el".' It meant 'The House of God'.

Jacob set off again. He travelled for many weeks. At last he came to the city of Haran where his uncle Laban lived.

Laban had two daughters. The elder one was called Leah. The younger one was called Rachel. Jacob soon fell in love with Rachel. He wanted to marry her but he did not have any money.

One day, when Jacob had been there for a month, Laban said to him, 'You are doing a lot of work for me on the farm. I should pay you some proper wages.'

Jacob thought quickly. 'I'll tell you what,' he said. 'I should like to marry Rachel but I haven't any money. I'll work for you for nothing for seven years if you will let me marry her and then give me sheep and goats so that I can afford to keep her.'

Laban agreed. The seven years passed very quickly. The day of the wedding came. Laban put on a big feast. There was a lot of food and wine. Everyone was dancing and having a good time.

As it got dark the bride was brought in. She wore a thick veil, as was the custom. The wedding took place. Then the dancing started again. It went on all night.

It wasn't until the morning that the bride took off her veil. Jacob nearly fainted with horror. It wasn't Rachel he had married. It was her elder sister, Leah. Jacob did not know what to do. He had been tricked. He went to see Laban.

'Why have you done this to me?' he asked.

'I thought you liked tricks,' said Laban. 'You used to play them on your brother Esau when you took his birthright and his blessing.'

27

Jacob did not like it but he knew it was true. What could he do?

Laban came to the rescue. 'I'll tell you what I will do,' he said. 'If you promise to work for me for another seven years you can marry Rachel as well – next week.'

Another seven years! It was a long time. But it would be worth it. Jacob agreed.

Laban did not trick him again. He had no more elder daughters to get rid of. Jacob married Rachel. He worked for Laban for another seven years. Above all he had learned a lesson. The time had come to go home and to make peace with his brother Esau. Would Esau still want to kill him? He did not know. But he knew he did not hate Esau any more and he could not stay away for ever. He got ready to go.

ABOUT THE STORY

The well-known Jacob's Ladder dream at Bethel possesses surrealist qualities – a point to be borne in mind if considering art work in connection with this story. Jacob himself is part of the means by which heaven and earth interrelate. We have here too the notion of sacred place. The word 'holy' means 'separate, put aside'. It possesses some awesome transcendental quality and was often associated with fear.

By contrast the ensuing Laban incident is a good 'come-uppance' story, not lacking self-deprecating humour. Jacob the deceiver is deceived. Anger is followed by resignation from which, in turn, comes the realization of what he has done to his brother. Desire for reconciliation arises out of imaginative understanding. He now knows what it feels like. It is experience rather than rational explanation which convinces.

Unlike Isaac, Jacob returns to the ancestral home, the final link with Haran. Are there hints here too about the wisdom of experience contrasted with the enthusiasm of youth? Are Jacob's attempts at finding his own wife as successful as Eliezer's earlier quest for Isaac's? Polygamy, it needs to be noted, is automatically accepted in a society where the single woman has no place. Laban is to be seen as working for the best interests of his daughters. The great questions of the struggle of women to be equal partners are all inherent in these four-thousand-year-old stories.

The journey motif continues to be strong and it exists at two levels. In returning to his roots Jacob is searching for himself.

IDEAS FOR EXPLORING FURTHER

Holy Places   Discuss what may happen in a place to make it feel 'holy' or 'special'. Why do people make long pilgrimages or gather at particular sites at certain times of the year? Find out about Christian holy places such as Lourdes, St Peter's Church in Rome, Glastonbury, Canterbury. Discover why Muslims visit Medina and Makkah. Learn about the value of the River Ganges and Benares to Hindus, the significance of Amritsar to Sikhs and of Jerusalem to several religious traditions. (See Story 38.)

Dreams and Reality   Make links between fantasy and reality, dreams and real life, indicating how dreams and fantasy often symbolize and reflect aspects of people's lives such as searching for meaning to life; trying to understand the mysteries of life; looking for a source of strength to help overcome evil; struggling to solve a problem; trying to find God. Extracts from fiction which highlight journeying and sacred places could be used to reinforce these ideas (e.g. the traditional tale of Baboushka; *The Hobbit*, by J. R. R. Tolkien; the Narnia stories by C. S. Lewis; *The Wizard of Earthsea*, by Ursula LeGuin; *The Heartstone Odyssey*, by Arvan Kumar; *Pangur Ban*, by Fay Sampson).

6

A Wrestling-match

Genesis 32: 3 – 33: 12

Jacob was frightened. He had made the long journey back through the desert and tomorrow he would meet Esau. Would his brother still want to kill him?

It looked rather like it. A few days ago he had sent messengers on ahead to tell Esau he was coming. When they had come back he had asked them, 'How did my brother take the news that I am coming?' The messengers had replied, 'He has gathered four hundred men and is coming out to meet you.'

It seemed as if Esau wanted to fight after all. Jacob had lots of people with him but he did not want to fight. So he had divided all his goats and sheep and camels into three groups. He had sent them off one group at a time, ahead of him and his family. He had told the man in charge of each group, 'When my brother meets you, tell him that all these animals are a present from me to him.'

Finally, he had been left with his two wives Leah and Rachel and all his children. Tonight they had come to the River Jabbok, which was the boundary of the land. He had sent his family across the ford and had stayed behind. Now he was all alone – or at least he thought he was.

Jacob lay down and looked up at the stars. It was just like the night many years before when he had had that strange dream of a ladder at Bethel. This might be his last night on earth. Perhaps tomorrow Esau would kill him.

Suddenly, Jacob knew he was not on his own. There was somebody else there. The night was dark. The desert air was cold. Jacob tossed and turned on the ground. He was fighting another man. All through the night the two wrestled with one another. Neither would give way. The fight was so real that Jacob's hip was put out of joint.

Daylight came. Had it all been just a dream? There was no one to be seen but the feeling that the other man was still there was very strong. 'Don't go away,' gasped Jacob. 'Stay here and give me a blessing.' From deep down inside him came a voice. It asked, 'Who are you?'

It seemed a silly question. It was easy simply to say 'Jacob' – but who was he really? The trouble was that there were two Jacobs. There was Jacob the deceiver, the one who had tricked his brother. But there was also the other Jacob, the loyal, honest Jacob who had been deceived himself but had remained loyal to Leah even though he did not like her. Which one was the real him?

The voice came to him again. It said, 'You shall have a new name. You shall no longer be called Jacob. From now on you will be known as Israel.'

It was a good name. It meant 'one who has struggled with God and has found his real self'. It was as if there had been two people in one, always fighting one another.

'Tell me,' said Jacob aloud. 'Who are you?'

'You don't need to know my name,' came the answer.

Jacob knew without any doubt that it was God.

Jacob got up. Down the hill on the other side of the river came his brother Esau with his four hundred men. This was the moment he had been dreading. Now, he suddenly realized, he wasn't frightened any more. He felt at peace with himself and with Esau. He was not frightened of dying.

Esau crossed the ford of the river and ran towards Jacob. Jacob waited. For the first time in many years the two brothers faced one another.

'What are all these presents of animals for?' asked Esau.

'They are to ask you to forgive me,' replied Jacob.

31

Esau laughed. But it was a kind laugh. 'I've plenty of my own,' he said. 'Come on, let us learn to live together again.' The two brothers crossed the river together as friends. The children of Israel could grow up in the land of Canaan.

NOTES

ABOUT THE STORY

There are at least two themes in this very profound story. It is, first of all, a crisis narrative, an account of what may happen when we are compelled to face up to what we really are. There is a background of real fear and an inability any longer to avoid the consequences of previous actions. The mood is akin to that created by, for example, Ursula LeGuin in *The Wizard of Earthsea* when Ged is brought to the point of facing and naming the shadow. That work alone shows that although this account belongs to the realm of adulthood and relates to conflict with the *alter ego*, the dark night of the soul and the light of dawn, it is, nevertheless, an experience not by any means unknown in childhood.

The second theme is concerned with the nature of Israel, the people of God. The weak, immature and deceitful Jacob has another side to him if he will but recognize and acknowledge it. When it is acknowledged he becomes the vehicle through which the Divine is made known. The transcendent emerges triumphant from his struggle with the base material of his day-to-day existence. The change is such as to bring about a change of identity and, therefore, of name. He *becomes* Israel. Today we are very casual about our use of names. This is a relatively modern departure but one exception is those entering the religious life, where still a change of name is bound up with the idea of taking on a new identity.

The return to Canaan marks the final departure from a previous home and culture. Abraham may be seen as the father of the race but the children of Israel, as he must now be called, are to be a new nation, a separate (holy) people.

IDEAS FOR EXPLORING FURTHER

What's In a Name?   Provide information about the origin and meaning of names of people and places. (Parents can often give valuable information to supplement reference books.) A survey may reveal factors about name-giving. Let pupils choose a new name for themselves or someone else. Ask for reasons behind decisions. Look at newspaper births columns to see popular names for children at present. Contrast these with names from gravestones entered into a data base. (■ *Information Technology*) Older pupils could consider why some names are more common than others. Discuss the 99 names of Allah, and compare with names for God used by other traditions.

A Good Self and a Bad Self   Discuss with older children how and why people with faith try to use their higher nature to make the world a better place. Sometimes we know we have done wrong and need to make amends. Take examples from school, home and work. Discuss stories in books, on TV and video about people tempted by their lower self and describe consequences. Making amends may require a greater or lesser degree of struggle and may be followed by fine actions. Why is it so hard to say 'Sorry' and is it important? Very often, people do not like being at odds with each other. Ask what pupils feel when they are angry with people. What causes rifts? What would solve problems? How do they feel when they are friends again? Try to express emotions and moods through exploring single sounds and sound patterns.

7

Getting Rid of a Boastful Brother

Genesis 37

Jacob had twelve sons, of whom Joseph was his favourite. Ten of the sons were older than Joseph. One was younger. But they all hated Joseph because their father loved him best. Jacob (or Israel, as he was now also called) had given Joseph a special cloak. All the other brothers had ordinary shepherds' cloaks with no sleeves. Joseph's had long, wide sleeves and was woven from wool of many colours.

Joseph was a dreamer. That only made things worse. If only he could have kept quiet about his dreams it wouldn't have mattered, but he was a boaster as well.

One day he said to his brothers, 'I had a dream last night.'

The brothers groaned.

'I'll tell you about it,' said Joseph.

'Surprise, surprise,' said one of the brothers.

Joseph ignored him and went on. 'We were all in the fields. It was harvest time. We were tying up sheaves of corn. Suddenly my sheaf stood up on end and all your sheaves came round in a circle and bowed down to it.' He grinned at his brothers.

'Who do you think you are?' shouted one of the eleven. 'Do you think we're ever going to bow down to you?'

'Stop it!' called Jacob. 'He's only young. He will grow up.'

But even Jacob got angry next time Joseph told them of a dream.

'It was like this,' said Joseph. 'I was standing outside, looking up at the sky. There were the sun and the moon and eleven stars. As I watched they all formed a circle and bowed down to me.'

'Are you saying that your mother and I are going to bow down to you?' shouted Jacob. 'Really, you are painful to listen to.'

'Now you know how we feel,' said Joseph's brothers.

Jacob shook his head. He was angry, but there was something strange about young Joseph. He didn't like the dream but he knew he would remember it.

One day Jacob sent for Joseph. 'Go and find your brothers,' he said. 'They have been out with the sheep for several days. Go and see if they are all right.'

Joseph set off. After many hours of searching he saw them in the distance. They saw him too. He had his multicoloured coat on. They could recognize him easily.

'Look who's coming – and all alone too. Now's our chance. Let's get rid of him once and for all.'

'Good idea. Come on. Down behind these rocks.'

They lay in ambush. As Joseph came past they jumped out on him and began hitting him.

Suddenly close at hand a voice roared, 'Stop it, you fools, stop it!'

It was Reuben, the eldest brother. He had been away looking for a sheep at the other end of the valley. 'You can't kill a brother, whatever he's done,' Reuben went on. 'Push him in the pit while we think what to do with him.'

Grumbling to themselves the other brothers pushed Joseph into the lion-trap, a deep hole usually covered with branches. He couldn't climb out. Joseph didn't care. Reuben would rescue him later. He knew that.

'Look, more visitors coming!'

It was Judah who spoke. The others looked up. A line of camels was coming towards them. It was a caravan of merchants on their way to Egypt. Judah looked round. Reuben had gone off again to look for the missing sheep.

'That's it,' exclaimed Judah. 'Let's sell Joseph. Then we can get rid of him without killing him, and make some money at the same time.'

The merchants came by. The caravan stopped.

'Do you want to buy a slave?' asked Judah. 'He's young, good-looking and strong. He will fetch a good price in Egypt. You can have him for thirty shekels.'

The brothers dragged Joseph out of the pit. He was bruised and dirty. The merchants looked at him. 'We'll give you ten shekels,' they said.

The brothers began to argue. In the end Joseph was sold for twenty shekels without his cloak. The brothers kept that. A rope was tied round Joseph's hands and then to a camel. He went away half walking, half being pulled.

Reuben came back. He passed the pit. It was empty. 'Where's Joseph?' he asked.

'It's all right, we haven't killed him. We've sold him. Here you are. We've kept your share of the money.'

'You idiots,' screamed Reuben, knocking the money on to the ground. 'Have you thought what you are going to tell our father, Jacob? He will kill us if he finds out.'

They hadn't thought of that at all. Then they had an idea. They took Joseph's cloak and tore it up. One of the brothers killed a goat and spread some of the blood on the torn wool. A few days later they went home.

'Where is Joseph?' asked Jacob as soon as he met them. 'I sent him to find you.'

'We haven't seen him,' lied Reuben. 'But we did wonder, because we found this on the way home.' He held out the remains of the torn cloak.

After that no one could cheer Jacob up. He wept and wept for Joseph. He was quite convinced that his favourite son had been killed and eaten by wild animals.

Meanwhile, hundreds of miles away, Joseph was being sold again in an Egyptian slave-market. This time he was bought by a man called Potiphar. Potiphar was an officer of the royal bodyguard of the Pharaoh of Egypt.

ABOUT THE STORY

The story of Joseph is of a rather unusual form for biblical literature. It is a colourful saga of great length, full of high drama but lacking in the intensity of some of the earlier stories. Perhaps it is for this reason that it has captured popular imagination right down to the present day. There is a certain pantomime quality about it. To retain some measure of consistency it is told here in four instalments of roughly equal length.

One of the functions of the whole story would appear to be that of linking the stories of the Patriarchs with the sharper historical narratives connected with Moses. Something had to account for the otherwise sudden appearance of the Israelites in Egypt.

The other emphasis is that Joseph's God is with him wherever he goes. God is in his head, the source of his insight and later wisdom.

As with the earlier story of Jacob, the ultimate hero of this tale is first of all shown in a very unfavourable light. Again he has cleverness but no wisdom; again he is a younger brother, and again he is a parental favourite. He is gifted but arrogant, privileged to stay at home while the other brothers toil in some discomfort. Any justification for his boastful claims lies in the future. Sympathy is with the older brothers until they overstep the mark. There is human frailty all round, no 'goodies and baddies', but Joseph is transformed in the process of growing up.

The Bible account is made up of at least two interwoven sources in which the traders are variously Ishmaelites and Midianites, with other similar discrepancies. This retelling attempts to blend the strands into one narrative by avoiding the precise details found in the biblical text.

IDEAS FOR EXPLORING FURTHER

Egypt   Make links with ▉▉ *History*: SSU – Ancient Egypt. Discuss the fact that no other written evidence has been found of the presence of Joseph or his family in Egypt. (▉▉ *History*: AT 2) This story and the following three provide information on the Pharaoh and famines threatening Egyptian communities. Make links with ▉▉ *Science*: the rain cycle; climate and farming; *Geography*: AT 3 – weather conditions in different parts of the world, landforms, erosion, weathering, river systems; AT 4 – population density, journeys, transport, land use; AT 1 – map work on ancient trade routes of the Middle East.

Sensitivity towards Others   Use shadow, sock or stick puppets with extracts from 'Joseph and His Amazing Technicolour Dreamcoat', by Andrew Lloyd Webber, to emphasize how characters were sensitive or not to the well-being of others. Length of dialogue can be varied, with a narrator bearing the burden of the story if necessary. (▉▉ *English*: AT 1)

8

Someone Must Know What My Dreams Are All About

Genesis 39: 20 – 41: 15

Joseph was in Egypt. He was a slave and he was in prison. It wasn't his fault. Potiphar had been a good man and Joseph had enjoyed working for him. It was Potiphar's wife who had been the trouble. Telling all those lies about him. That's why he was in prison – and who cared about slaves? He didn't know what was going to happen to him. Perhaps he would just stay there until he died.

Suddenly the prison door opened. It was the prison governor.

'Come with me, Joseph,' he ordered. 'I have a job for you.'

The governor led Joseph to a different part of the prison. He opened the door of another cell. Two men were inside.

'Look after these two,' said the governor. 'They are special prisoners of Pharaoh.'

One of the prisoners had been Pharaoh's butler. The other had been his baker. Both of them had the job of seeing that nobody tried to poison Pharaoh. They were important prisoners. Joseph did all the dirty jobs for them like sweeping out their cell. What else could a slave expect?

One morning he went in as usual. The two men looked white. They were shaking all over.

'What's the matter?' asked Joseph.

'We've had bad dreams,' said the butler, 'and no one can tell us what they are all about.'

'Try me,' said Joseph. 'I'm pretty good at dreams.'

The two men looked at each other. Then the butler spoke.

'In my dream,' he said, 'I saw a vine. It had three branches. All in a flash the buds burst into blossom and the blossom turned into grapes. I picked them, squeezed them straight into wine, poured it into a goblet and took it in to Pharaoh. It all happened as quick as lightning. Then I woke up.'

There was a silence. Joseph closed his eyes. Then he opened them again and smiled.

'It's good news,' he said. 'The three branches are three days and in that time you will be set free. You will go back to the palace and be Pharaoh's butler again. Just remember me when you get there, won't you?'

'Oh yes,' said the butler, looking very pleased.

'My dream was a bit like that,' interrupted the baker. 'I had three bread baskets on my head. In the top one were lots of freshly baked loaves and cakes for the Pharaoh. But as I walked along birds kept swooping down and pecking at them. I couldn't keep them away. Will I get out in three days as well?'

There was another silence. Then Joseph shook his head. When he spoke his voice was very sad.

'Your dream is just the opposite,' he said. 'The three baskets mean three days, all right. But in three days' time it is you the birds will be eating. Pharaoh has decided to have you executed.'

Pharaoh's birthday was three days later. It all happened as Joseph had said. The baker was taken out and hanged for trying to poison Pharaoh. The butler was set free. As he went, Joseph said again, 'Remember me.'

'Of course,' said the butler. But he forgot. Joseph stayed in prison. Two years passed.

Pharaoh was in a bad mood. All his servants were frightened when he was in one of these tempers. It was all the fault of his wise men this time. What were they paid for?

Pharaoh banged on the arm of his throne and shouted at them again. 'Fools, fools, I'll have you all thrown to the crocodiles. I am served by idiots. My dreams are very clear. They had fat cows and thin cows, fat grains of corn and thin grains of corn in them. Surely that's simple enough. And yet you sit there like lumps of stone. Someone must know what my dreams are all about.'

Behind the throne stood the butler. Suddenly he remembered. He leaned forward.

'Your Majesty,' he whispered, 'I once knew a man who could tell the meaning of dreams.'

'Where is he now?' demanded Pharaoh, still very angry.

'In your prison, Your Majesty,' replied the butler. He went on to tell him all about Joseph, his own dream and that of the baker.

'Bring him here at once,' ordered Pharaoh.

Soldiers were sent down to the prison. Joseph was pulled out into the bright sunlight. His prison rags were stripped off him and a clean robe was placed over his shoulders. 'Where are you taking me?' he asked.

'To the Pharaoh,' said one of the soldiers. 'You're going to tell him what his dreams are all about or else ....'

He didn't finish the sentence, but the other soldiers laughed. They took Joseph straight to the palace.

ABOUT THE STORY

The dream motif occurs again and again. However, here the treatment is relatively shallow and the interpretative procedure comes over as very mechanical. For example, there is a total absence of the agonizing mental struggle pointed to in the Jacob stories, even though lives, the butler's and the baker's, are at stake here. There is an almost casual jollity about the whole episode and the minor characters are very two-dimensional, almost cartoon figures, who seem to exist in the story solely to highlight the supposed virtues of Joseph himself. Treatment can justifiably be quite light.

At the same time there is a genuinely religious theme in that Joseph's God, contrary to all appearances, is in charge of all that is happening.

Perhaps the one point which is close to social reality is the arbitrary nature of justice in some parts of the ancient world (and, for that matter, in parts of our own world). There is something of a 'Mikado' quality about Pharoah's style of decision-making. This does not in any way invalidate the story as moral literature. What it does is to give it childlike qualities. The issues are presented in stark black and white terms and the punishments, as often in the play of young children, are harsh and severe.

IDEAS FOR EXPLORING FURTHER

Recognizing One's Gifts   To foster self-esteem, ask pupils to say or write down one sentence about themselves and/or another person along the lines of 'I/X have/has the gift of...' to encourage discussion about differing gifts. Emphasize qualities such as being a good listener, having the ability to share, knowing how to be kind to others, etc.

Justice and Fair Play   Talk about everyday experiences, e.g. telling lies, equal access to toys, materials, sports, jobs. With older children, use the story as a starting-point to discuss citizenship issues. (NC Citizenship) What different kinds of society are/were there in history? What does/did it mean to have a strong authoritarian ruler? What does it mean to be a citizen in multi-ethnic Britain or other localities today? What kinds of rights do people have? Are rights balanced by responsibilities? Take up the theme of rights and differing concepts of fairness as part of a local study or in relation to world issues and current news items. (NC History: social, cultural, religious aspects; Geography: ATs 2, 5) Make or collect pictures/articles about injustice, mount them on a corridor wall and leave free space for children to ask questions or to comment.

41

9

You Are the Man to Do It

Genesis 41: 6 – 42: 8

Pharaoh sat on the golden throne. All around him stood his courtiers and servants. The room was full and everyone was silent. In front of Pharaoh stood Joseph. Only an hour or so ago he had been in prison. Now as he stood there everyone was looking at him. Inside he shook with fear.

Pharaoh looked up. 'So,' his voice rang out, 'you can tell what dreams are all about, can you?'

There was silence again. Joseph found his voice at last. He spoke up clearly. 'It's not me,' he said. 'It's my God inside me. I am just his spokesman. But first tell me your dreams.'

'There were two dreams,' replied Pharaoh. 'In the first I was standing by the River Nile. As I watched, seven cows came up out of the water. They came to the bank and started to eat the grass. All of them were fat with soft, glossy skins. Then another seven cows came out of the water. They were very thin and scraggy. To my surprise as they came out of the water they turned and ate up the seven fat cows. The funny thing was that they didn't get any fatter themselves.'

Pharaoh paused. Then he went on: 'The second dream was very like the first, only this time I was in a field of corn. I saw a stalk with seven big fat ears of corn on it. Then as I watched another seven thin dry ears appeared on the stalk. They ate up the juicy ones in a flash. But they didn't get any bigger themselves either.'

Pharaoh leaned forward and looked straight at Joseph.

42

'Now,' he said, 'tell me what it's all about. I hope you can do better than these fools.' He waved his hand towards a group of his wise men. They looked scared.

Joseph did not hesitate. 'Both of your dreams mean the same thing,' he said. 'The seven fat cows and the seven fat ears of corn mean that Egypt will have seven good harvests. The seven thin cows and the seven thin ears of corn mean that they will be followed by seven very bad harvests. When that time comes, you and your people will starve, unless ...' Joseph paused.

Pharaoh leaned forward again. 'Unless what?' he asked quietly.

'Unless,' said Joseph, 'you stop people from eating too much in the good years so that they save food for the bad years. People will want to enjoy themselves when they have a lot. It will need a strong man to stop them and make them save. The food will have to be put into stores and guarded. Then it will have to be given out very carefully in the bad years.'

There was a silence. Pharaoh spoke again. What he said nearly made Joseph faint with surprise.

'Excellent,' said Pharaoh. 'And you are the man to do it.' He turned to the courtiers who were nearby. 'This man shall be the second most important person in Egypt after me,' he said. 'His chariot shall come just behind mine. Everybody will take orders from him.' He turned to Joseph. 'You are in charge,' he said.

As if from nowhere servants appeared. Joseph, who only an hour before had been a forgotten slave in prison, found himself dressed in silk clothes with gold rings on his fingers. He had a palace to live in, a chariot to drive in and dozens of servants to look after him.

It all happened as Joseph had said. For seven years he made sure that lots of food was collected. He had barns built and guards placed in front of them. Many people grumbled as one good harvest followed another and still they were not allowed to have more food than normal.

Then in the eighth year the harvest failed. There was no food. People began to starve. Joseph opened up the barns. Very carefully he gave out the corn. It had to last for seven years.

Another year passed and another bad harvest. In other countries people were starving. Travellers started to come to Egypt because they heard there was food there.

One day a large group of men came from Canaan. There were ten of them. They bowed low in front of Joseph. The eldest one spoke.

'Oh, noble prince,' he said, 'help us. Our family is starving. Allow us to buy food from you.'

Joseph gasped. He knew that voice. It was his brother Reuben. The last time he had heard it was when his brothers had thrown him into a pit before selling him into slavery. He looked closely at the group. They were all older but he recognized them all. Only Benjamin, the youngest, was missing – and where was his father?

Joseph decided to find out. He would play a trick on them.

ABOUT THE STORY

Joseph's dramatic change of fortune comes about through his skills as an interpreter of dreams. He has nothing else to offer except his insights which come from deep within him but there is no denying the source. For all their prestige and power the soothsayers of Pharaoh cannot begin to compete with the inspiration which comes from Joseph's God.

By the end of this section of the story Joseph is the Pharaoh's right-hand man, his fortunes suddenly reversed in the best traditions of comic opera.

However, such known traditions as lie behind this whole saga suggest that close relationships between the Hebrews in Egypt and their rulers was quite possible. The Hyksos or Shepherd Kings who ruled Egypt between 3600 and 3800 years ago are thought to have been from a tribe of the same stock as the Hebrews, and it is reasonable to assume that the Habiru, as they were called, were not unwelcome guests. The arrival of the ten brothers, the clan chiefs, at the end of this episode may well suggest that there was significant movement into Egypt because of widespread famine. Compare modern migrations in Saharan Africa at times of famine.

Nevertheless, the story continues in its now familiar form. It is primarily to be told with enjoyment in mind, with its sudden twists of fate and reversal of roles communicating, albeit in comic form, many serious ideas.

IDEAS FOR EXPLORING FURTHER

Seeking God's Strength and Using It   Read stories from different traditions showing how people have been inspired by God's strength and power, have overcome obstacles and done important work (e.g. Guru Nanak, Muhammad, David, Gideon). Compare with the more recent past and today (e.g. the Jamaican Mary Seacole, Crimea companion to Florence Nightingale, Martin Luther King, Mother Teresa). Find out about Hindu respect for Ganesha.

Famine   Discuss what causes it. (NC Cf. notes to Story 7.) What choices are open to sufferers and onlookers? Why do some people decide to help and others refuse? For example, Bob Geldof did much to raise money for poor people. Why did he feel this was important? What does he seem to value? Juniors could play 'The World Feast Game', a simulation concerning world food production, available from Christian Aid, P.O. Box 100, London SE1 7RT.

10

Israel Goes to Egypt

Genesis 42: 9 – 46: 7

Once Joseph had had a dream. In it his brothers' sheaves of corn had bowed down to his in the harvest field. Now it had come true. Ten of his brothers were on their knees in front of him. They did not know who he was. They had sold him as a slave. Now he was a prince in Egypt, second only to Pharaoh. He would play a trick on them. He spoke.

'You are spies,' said Joseph. 'You have come here to spy on us so that you can come and steal our corn.'

'No, no,' cried the brothers. 'We are all from one family. We are eleven sons of the same father.'

'Eleven?' asked Joseph. 'I see only ten. Where is the other?'

'Our father would not let him travel with us,' answered Reuben.

'Why not?' asked Joseph.

'Once we were twelve,' replied Reuben. 'But our younger brother, who was our father's favourite, was killed. Now our father will not let the youngest son travel with us.'

Joseph went on asking questions. Somehow he had to make sure that they would come back and bring the youngest brother, Benjamin, with them. He also wanted to see his father Jacob, or Israel, as he was known. At last he said, 'I will let nine of you go. The other will stay here as a hostage until you come back with this other brother to show you are telling the truth.'

One brother, Simeon, was put in prison. The others set off back home with their sacks of corn. When they got home they each found money in their corn sacks. They were frightened. It looked as if they had not paid for the corn.

Jacob was angry when he heard the story. 'Why did you tell him about Benjamin?' he asked.

'Because he asked so many questions,' replied Reuben. 'He seemed to know so much that we could not outwit him.'

A year passed. The food began to run out again. Jacob spoke to his sons.

'You must travel to Egypt again,' he said. 'Take twice as much money as before to show you did not steal.' Sadly he agreed that Benjamin would have to go with them.

When they got back to Egypt the brothers were surprised at the welcome they received. No one asked about money. Instead they were given a great feast at Joseph's palace. All the time Joseph asked questions about them and their father.

Had they known what was happening while they ate and talked, they would have been very unhappy. Joseph had given orders to his servants. 'Fill their sacks with corn,' he had said, 'and then put one of my silver goblets in Benjamin's sack.'

Next morning the brothers set off with their heavy loads. They had not travelled far when they heard a noise behind them. Looking back they saw Egyptian soldiers bearing down on them in chariots.

'Stop!' commanded the officer. 'You are under arrest. One of you has stolen a precious silver goblet from our High Steward.'

The brothers could not believe their ears.

'Search us,' they cried.

The soldiers did. In Benjamin's sack they found the silver goblet. The brothers were very frightened indeed as they were led back as prisoners.

Once again they stood in front of Joseph. He tried to look angry. He shouted, 'Benjamin must be punished.'

'This will kill our father,' said Reuben. 'Let Benjamin go back. We will stay here and be punished for him even though we are innocent. We cannot let our father suffer again.'

They began to tell Joseph the story of how they had sold him as a slave. They told him how they had lied to Jacob and how he had cried and cried. On and on they talked.

At last Joseph could not stand it any longer. He held up his hands for silence. 'I am your brother Joseph,' he said. 'Do you not recognize me?'

The brothers gasped. Could it be true? Surely he would kill them all now.

Instead Joseph put his arms round them all in turn. 'I was angry once,' he said. 'But see how it has worked out. Surely I was made to come to Egypt so that our family, Israel and all his children might be saved. Go and get Israel, our father. Bring him to Egypt. We shall live here together.'

So Israel came to Egypt. He lived there with his twelve sons and died there. Because of all that Joseph had done, the Pharaoh allowed the children of Israel to have land and to settle in Egypt.

The story of Joseph is the story of how the children of Israel came to live in Egypt. Once they had been desert travellers, or Hebrews as they were called. Now they came to be known as Israelites.

In time Joseph and all his brothers died. But their children and their grandchildren lived on. The number of Israelites grew and grew. For hundreds of years they lived in Egypt – until there came to the throne a Pharaoh who had never heard of Joseph.

ABOUT THE STORY

Within the drawn-out *dénouement* we are given one of the main threads of the Joseph saga. Israel (Jacob) comes to settle in Egypt with his sons, who are to be the founders of the twelve tribes.

The practical joke played out over a year or more has, once again, something of the quality of farce: the audience knows the true identity of Joseph, the characters do not. There is pathos but there is also humour. It is entertaining but it is also morally instructive. The brothers are made to suffer until they make a full and complete confession. Then there is total forgiveness and reconciliation.

As we shall see, the ten tribes which later formed the Northern Kingdom (Story 28) eventually disappeared from the pages of history. Benjamin is separated from the other brothers by Joseph. It was the tiny, two-tribe Kingdom of Judah, of which the tribe of Benjamin was a part, which survived and became the remnant out of which modern Judaism was to emerge. Whoever *wrote* this story would have known this.

IDEAS FOR EXPLORING FURTHER

Intercultural Enrichment   Make a list of the contributions made by people of different religions and cultures to the local, regional, national and international community (e.g. medicine, science, business, education, art, music, song, drama, sport, literature, fashion, jewellery, food). Make a collection of artefacts, pictures, written articles, things to taste, sing, listen to, etc. (Cf. Stories 11, 12, 18, 39, 40, 41.)

Use and Misuse of Power   (Cf. Story 28.) Discuss the responsibility that goes with power. What values lie behind how power is used? Talk about use/misuse of power in fiction, today or in the past. (NC *History*: CSU 2 – Tudor and Stuart times; CSU 4 – Second World War; CSU 6 – destruction of indigenous peoples through voyages of discovery) What is the role of leaders in the management of world resources? (NC *Economic and Industrial Understanding*; *Geography*: ATs 2, 4, 5 – provision of goods and services in a local economy; planning and the environment)

49

11

Spare the Girls but Kill the Boys

Exodus 1: 8 – 2: 10

Egypt had a new Pharaoh. As he looked around he saw lots of foreigners in his country.

'Where did all these people come from?' he asked.

His advisers tried to explain.

'About four hundred years ago, Your Majesty, one of their ancestors called Joseph was brought here as a slave. He had a gift for telling the meaning of dreams. Egypt was saved from famine and starvation because of him. The Pharaoh of the time rewarded him by letting his family live in Egypt for ever.'

Pharaoh listened. Then he said, 'I know nothing of this Joseph. It is all too long ago. These people are a nuisance now. There are too many of them. Make them slaves. Put them to work. They can build my new cities and work on the pyramids.'

And so it happened. The Israelites became slaves. They were forced to live in slave-camps and to do all the heavy and dirty work without any wages. They dragged the huge building stones from the quarries to the work sites. In the fields they worked from dawn till dusk. If they did not work hard enough they were whipped.

Many died, but still their numbers grew. More and more Israelite babies were born. Pharaoh got more and more worried. Finally he issued an order. It said: 'When babies are born to the Israelite women the girls shall be allowed to live. The boys will be thrown in the river. Spare the girls but kill the boys.'

A shudder of horror ran through the Israelite camps.

One family in particular was frightened. Already they had a daughter of twelve called Miriam, and a boy of three called Aaron. Another baby was expected any day. It was a boy. What could be done? It was not possible to hide a baby for very long, especially during the daytime. For three months they managed. Then the mother had an idea.

The Israelite camp was on the bank of the River Nile. The edge of the river was full of reeds and bulrushes. The woman took some reeds and wove them into a basket. She covered it inside and out with tar. When it was finished it was both a cradle and a boat. Pushed out among the bulrushes at the water's edge, where there was no current, it should be perfectly safe. Surely no one would think of looking there.

The next time soldiers came near the camp the woman hurried down to the water with the floating cradle. She put her plan into action. It worked. The cradle floated but it did not move.

The woman waited until the soldiers had gone. Then she set off back to the river. She felt happy. Her baby was safe. Or was he? She froze in horror. There, just at the spot where she had placed the cradle, stood a small group of people. They seemed to be all women. What were they doing? It looked as if they were searching for somewhere to swim.

It was one of the daughters of Pharaoh himself. As the woman watched from a distance she heard the princess speak.

'Find me somewhere where there are no reeds. I will wait here,' she said.

She sat down with one or two friends while the servants went off along the river bank. Suddenly she looked up. 'What was that?' she said.

'I heard nothing, Your Highness,' replied her friend.

'Listen. There was a noise from the river. There it is again.'

A little way away the mother went white with fear. She had heard the noise too. A little whimper. Her baby had been there for some time. He would be getting hungry.

Suddenly the whimper turned into a full baby cry. The

51

princess jumped to her feet. Her maid slid into the water and almost disappeared in the rushes. She came back pushing the basket on the water.

The baby's mother had started to run. She dashed back to the camp and caught her daughter. 'Quickly, Miriam,' she gasped, 'go and see what you can do.' She explained what was happening. Miriam ran off.

Miriam arrived to find a group of women round the baby. She heard the princess say, 'It's one of the Israelite babies. My father is too cruel sometimes. I'd adopt it myself, but I haven't got time to look after it.'

Miriam interrupted. She had squeezed to the front. 'Please, Your Highness. I could find a nurse if that would help.'

The princess turned round and looked at Miriam, who suddenly felt very small. Then the princess smiled and said, 'Good idea. Can you do it quickly?'

Within a few minutes Miriam returned with her mother. Nobody realized she was the baby's mother too. It was all arranged at once. The baby was to be brought up in the royal palace and his mother would be paid to be his nurse. As she took her own baby back to carry him to the palace, the mother asked the princess, 'Do you have a name for him?'

The princess thought for a moment and then said, 'Yes, I shall call him Moses because I found him in the water.'

NOTES

ABOUT THE STORY

It has often been said that if we had no records of the existence of Moses we should have had to invent him. With the Mosaic stories we start to move closer to recorded history. However, it is just at this point that we need to remind ourselves of what was said in the Introduction to this book. This is not just objective, detached history, if there ever were such a thing. It is history understood and told as the working-out of the sacred through the affairs and activities of men and women.

The well-known story of Moses in the bulrushes has been sentimentalized over the years. That distorts its truth. There is nothing very romantic about infanticide or the persecution of minority groups. A new dynasty had arisen. Tradition had been broken and anti-Semitic xenophobia was rife. The Hebrews were enslaved and their numbers were to be strictly controlled through a policy of culling. It is an old story but also a very modern one in a century like ours which has seen at least two such holocausts, in Armenia following the First World War and in Nazi Germany before and during the Second. The Kurds of Iraq are today in much the same position as these Hebrews in Egypt three thousand years ago.

All the more surprising then that this story is still told with something of a light touch. It is the young girl Miriam, the elder sister, who is the real hero of the piece and we see again the high value placed upon quick-wittedness. The threatened baby is not only rescued but becomes privileged, both reared in an Egyptian palace and yet brought up in the values and traditions of his own people by his Hebrew mother. He is saved for a purpose. It is the women who outwit those in power to bring this about.

IDEAS FOR EXPLORING FURTHER

Racial Discrimination   (Cf. Stories 10, 12, 18, 39, 40, 41.) Divide the class into two groups for any arbitrary reason: e.g. those who are/are not wearing blue today. Make the first group clear up or work longer just because they are in blue, while other pupils have an easier time. Reverse the roles. Reiterate the reason for the work allocation. Discuss how children felt in each role. Does it matter what we look like on the outside, what colour clothes, eyes, skin we have? What is important about people?

Heroines   (Cf. Stories 16, 40.) These tend to be forgotten. Look for important female characters within religious traditions. Talk about female leaders like Indira Gandhi and women with special qualities. (NC *History*: CSU 2 – Mary I, Elizabeth I, Mary Queen of Scots; CSU 3 – Queen Victoria, the Bronte sisters, Elizabeth Fry, Marie Curie; CSU 4 – women in the Second World War; CSU 6 – Queen Isabella of Castile; Marina amongst the Aztecs) Books sold by Letterbox Library (8 Bradbury Street, London N16 8JN; tel. 071-226-1633) challenge gender stereotypes and racial superiority.

Persecution   Many stories have been written about Jewish children being hidden from the Nazis in the Second World War. Compare with stories about Catholics, Protestants, Non-conformists being hidden during other periods. (NC *History*: CSU 2 – Tudor and Stuart times; CSU 4 – Second World War) Consider events in Ireland with older children.

12

The Call of Moses

Exodus 2: 11 – 3: 12; 4: 10–16

The whip cracked. The Israelite slave screamed. He fell to the ground. The Egyptian raised the whip above his head again. Suddenly it was snatched out of his hand from behind. At the same time an arm came round his throat and he began to choke. All the breath went out of him and he sank to the ground.

The slave still lay on the ground waiting for the whip to bite into his back again. When it did not happen he rolled over. There stood a tall, strong, well-dressed man. On the ground lay the slave-master, his broken whip a few metres away.

'Who are you?' gasped the slave.

'My name is Moses,' said the man. 'I too am an Israelite. But go quickly. Get to your feet and go.'

The slave got up.

'What about him?' he asked, pointing to the Egyptian.

'I think he is dead,' replied Moses. 'Hurry away. There is no one in sight. We must not be seen.'

The slave ran off. Moses hurried in the other direction.

Next day Moses was out again. This time he found two Israelites fighting each other. 'Stop that!' he shouted, and pushed them apart.

'Who do you think you are?' said one of the men angrily. 'I suppose you're going to kill me like you killed that Egyptian yesterday.'

Moses turned. 'What do you know about that?' he asked angrily.

The man looked frightened. Moses left him alone. He was frightened too.

That night Moses left Egypt. He walked for many days, which was just as well. When Pharaoh found out that his daughter's adopted son was really an Israelite he was very angry.

'Find him and bring him back,' he ordered his guards.

But Moses was too far away.

Moses travelled to the land of Midian. There he married a girl called Zipporah and became a shepherd. Every day he watched over the sheep which belonged to Zipporah's father. Many years passed by.

One day Moses was out as usual with the sheep. The sun was very hot. The sheep were scattered over the hillside. Suddenly Moses saw what seemed to be a bush on fire. It glowed, even in the sun. There was something strange about it. Moses felt frightened but he went nearer. The bush seemed to be on fire, but it wasn't burning away. It just glowed and glowed. Moses suddenly felt very frightened indeed.

From nowhere a voice came to him. It called his name: 'Moses, Moses.'

Moses stopped. 'Yes?' he stammered. 'Here I am.'

The voice spoke again. 'Do not come any closer,' it said. 'Take your shoes off. You are standing on holy ground.'

Moses did as he was told. The voice went on. 'I am God,' it said. 'I am the same God whom your ancestors worshipped.'

Moses was now very frightened. He pulled his arm over his face. He could not look at the bright light of the bush any more.

God spoke again. 'I know very well what is happening to my people in Egypt,' He said. 'It is time they were set free. I am going to send you to Pharaoh to rescue them.'

Moses found his voice again. 'Who am I to go to Pharaoh?' he asked. 'He will kill me.'

'No,' said God. 'I shall be with you and make you strong. When you have freed my people, bring them back here to this mountain.'

'But I'm no good at talking,' said Moses. 'I can never find the right words.'

God replied, 'I shall be with you. I shall put the words into your mouth.'

'O Lord,' said Moses. 'No, not me. Please send someone else.'

'You are the man I want,' came the answer. 'But if it makes you happier, take your brother Aaron with you. He can talk well enough. No more arguing.'

Moses knew he had to go. He went home, said goodbye to his wife and family and set off. He went first to find Aaron his brother to tell him what had happened. Together the two brothers set off back towards Egypt.

ABOUT THE STORY

The opening scene of this story is a labour camp, albeit without the high barbed-wire fences. It is a situation in which life is precarious and survival is the highest expectation one can hope for. It is from this that Moses escapes and to which he is later challenged to return.

This story has often been distorted in modern times by a literal emphasis on the bush. Here is a classic case of a story which can have come in the first instance only from the subject himself. He was on his own and later had to describe an intense spiritual experience which, against all his own inclinations, changed his life. It is a story of inner turmoil, of struggle and resistance. The bush plays some part but would a camera have shown anything? We cannot know. In moments of intense personal anguish the metaphor of burning springs readily to the lips whether it describes anger, frustration, desire or love.

Moses knows it is God with whom he is in conflict and in a typically Jewish manner he argues back. He does not want to go. Why should he? He has found safe refuge and is settled into a comfortable middle-class existence with wife, family and his own herds. He puts forward every excuse and each one is overruled. He has been born and bred for a purpose which must now be fulfilled. Note that Aaron is delegated to become his prophet – that is, his spokesman.

As with the patriarchal narratives Moses is a figure revered amongst Muslims as well as amongst Jews and Christians.

IDEAS FOR EXPLORING FURTHER

Bullying and Slavery   What was the difference between the Egyptian's and Moses' deed? Were they both forms of bullying? Talk about different forms of bullying inside school and outside. What are the reasons and results? Is doing nothing about bullying the same as condoning it? Help pupils to draw up a charter for how they wish all people to be treated (e.g. no name-calling, no cold-shouldering). Are adults being bullies when they mug or murder people? Is it a case of bullying when one country uses force to take over another and enslaves its people? (NC *History*: CSU 3 – Empire and slavery; CSU 6 – voyages of discovery) Most nations around the world have pluralist communities. If people do not have equal rights to land, homes and jobs, is that a form of bullying? (NC *Geography*: AT 2; *Citizenship*)

13

Let My People Go

Exodus 5: 1 – 12: 42

Moses and Aaron stood in front of Pharaoh.

'Let my people go,' said Moses. 'Our God demands it.'

'I do not know your God,' Pharaoh replied. 'And I do not care. What can the God of a bunch of slaves do against all the power of Egypt?'

'If you do not let my people go,' said Moses, 'the great River Nile will become like blood.'

Before Moses could say any more, Pharaoh called to his soldiers, 'Throw them out.'

Moses and Aaron were pushed out of the palace.

Next day the River Nile was a muddy reddish colour. The people of Egypt had nothing to drink and nothing with which to water their fields.

Nothing could live in the dirty river. The fish died. The frogs jumped out. They hopped everywhere as they looked for somewhere cool to hide. They got in the houses. They jumped into cooking-pots and water-jars. Even the beds and the food sacks were full of frogs. And they died when they could not find water to wet their skins.

The Egyptians piled up the dead frogs in the streets. The smell was everywhere and out came the flies. Millions and millions of them. The flies swarmed around the cattle and around people too. They brought disease and illness. Cattle died and people got sores and were sick.

All this time Moses and Aaron were going again and again

to see Pharaoh. Always Moses had the same thing to say, 'Let my people go. Our God demands it.'

But Pharaoh would not listen.

Moses tried again. 'If our people are still slaves at this time tomorrow,' he said, 'our God will send the biggest hailstorm you have ever seen.'

Pharaoh laughed.

Next day the laughing turned to crying. The hailstones were as big as tennis-balls. They flattened the corn, smashed through roofs of houses and knocked people over.

'Let my people go,' said Moses again.

'Never,' Pharaoh replied.

Then the locusts came like a great cloud in the sky. They blotted out the sun and landed on the fields. They ate all the rice and corn. Nothing was left. When harvest time came there would be no crops.

Pharaoh still would not release the slaves even when the sun was blotted out and there was darkness over the land for three whole days.

Finally Moses prepared for the last plague. He went to the slave-camps and gave orders. This was what he said:

'Take a lamb and on the fourteenth day of the month kill it. Take some of the blood and put it on the two doorposts and over the top of the door. Then go indoors and stay there. You shall make a meal of roast lamb and all the family will stay together.'

That night the Israelite camps were very quiet. Everyone was indoors. Something dreadful was going to happen.

At midnight there was an awful stillness. Suddenly from all the Egyptian houses came terrible crying. The eldest sons of all the Egyptians were dead, even the Pharaoh's own son.

Pharaoh did not wait for morning. He sent for Moses and Aaron. 'Get out!' he cried. 'Take your people with you. Take everything and go, as quickly as possible.'

Moses and Aaron did not wait. They hurried back to the slave-camps and gave orders. The Israelites were to leave their huts. They took only what they could carry. They took all the gold and jewellery they could find; there would be a use for that. Then they walked off into the desert, a strange long line of men, women and children. They did not know where they were going. At the front walked Moses and Aaron. They would go first to the mountain, the mountain where God had spoken to Moses. It would be a long march, as much as three months. And after that they would have to find a land in which to live. But somehow Moses knew that the God who had given the order would help them on the way.

NOTES

ABOUT THE STORY

The Exodus is one of the great central episodes of Jewish history. Its importance can hardly be exaggerated. At its very heart lies the notion of salvation. And yet it is a difficult story for non-Jews to tell with enthusiasm simply because, bound up in the story, along with the rejoicing at deliverance is the negative rejoicing at the plight of the Egyptians, seen in the suffering of the plagues, the terrible deaths of the first-born and the final destruction in whatever occurred at the Sea of Reeds. ('Red Sea' is now widely acknowledged to be a mistranslation.)

No doubt this is a natural reaction of any group set free after the most debasing forms of enslavement and maltreatment. In such circumstances we would all be likely to have become hardened and bitter. The problem comes from raising such natural emotions to the status of religious ideals and identifying all of them with images of God.

What is given here are those elements of the story which are most necessary for understanding the Jewish festival of Pesach (Passover). The emphasis is on that word. An alternative way to tell the whole story is to take the account from Deuteronomy 16 on how the Passover is to be kept. In its ritualized, rather than in its historical version, the Exodus is treated in a much more positive manner.

The plagues can be seen as arbitrary or as a natural sequence of events, at least up until the death of the first-born. Moses' courage takes the form of persistence. Whatever the historical details it is from this story that all ensuing biblical doctrines of deliverance and salvation develop. Whatever the outward facts the inner experience was decisive in Jewish and, later, in Christian development.

IDEAS FOR EXPLORING FURTHER

Freedom   Discuss difficult situations pupils have faced and the feelings after 'escape'. Consider Israelite reaction to the plagues, the Passover experience and leaving slavery. How had God helped them? Was it deserved? Discuss preparations for a long journey. What would Israelites pack? Imagine them looking outside. What would they hear? (E.g. crying, instructing, reminding.) What would they smell? (E.g. dead frogs/cattle, polluted river.) What would the physical constraints be? (E.g. fighting off flies, jostling, obstacles, mud after the hailstorm.) What would they see? (E.g. dead people/animals, flattened, empty fields.) After talking, let the class form 'families' and mime packing up. Ask each group in turn to make a tableau of their activities and to 'freeze'. A representative of Moses (child or teacher) then arrives to ask how they are getting on. Younger groups can say one line each about their readiness or reactions to what they have seen/heard, etc. Older ones can say more, creating a dramatic scene. The aim is to help children enter the inner experience of the situation, thereby gaining new insights and understanding about the meaning of the story. Good prior discussion is vital. (See also *Passover*, by Lynne Scholefield, Living Festivals series, RMEP.)

61

14

The Ten Rules – an Oath Signed in Blood

Exodus 19: 1 – 20: 20; 24: 3–8

Moses climbed up and up the mountain. A long way down below him he could see the rough tents of the Israelites. It was the mountain of God. This was where Moses had first met God, when he had seen the burning bush. It was here that he had heard God telling him to go to Egypt and rescue the Israelite slaves. The mountain was called Mount Sinai.

At the top of the mountain Moses felt God was near to him again.

'I am here, God,' said Moses. 'I have brought the people back as you told me to. What am I to do now?'

'Go back down the mountain,' said the voice of God. 'Tell the people that I am the God who rescued them from Egypt. Tell them that I want to make an agreement with them.'

'What sort of agreement?' asked Moses.

'This,' said God. 'I will go on being the God of the Israelites and looking after the people. In return the people must follow my ways.'

Moses went down the mountain. He called all the leaders of the people together. He told them what had happened on the mountain. Did they want to make an agreement – a solemn covenant with God? The people said they did.

Moses went up the mountain again. When he came back he carried the ten rules which were God's ways. They were carved in stone. Four of the rules told the people how they had to treat God. The other six told them how they had to behave to one another. These were the ten rules.

Duty to God
1. Do not have any other gods.
2. Do not make any images to worship.
3. Do not use God's name in wrong ways.
4. Do not work on the holy days.

Duty to One Another
5. Never look down on your parents.
6. Never murder.
7. Never run off with anybody else's wife or husband.
8. Never steal.
9. Never give other people a bad name.
10. Never be greedy for things which belong to other people.

A storm broke over the mountain. The lightning flashed; the thunder boomed; thick clouds whirled around. The mountain seemed to be covered in fire and smoke. In the middle of it all the ground shook. It was an earthquake.

All the people were frightened.

'This God comes in storms and earthquakes,' they said. 'This is a holy mountain. We must not touch it.'

'Will you accept these rules?' asked Moses.

'Yes, we will,' replied the people.

'We will swear it in blood,' replied Moses, 'to make it a solemn oath.'

He set to work. He built a great altar. Around it he built twelve tall pillars of stone, one for each tribe. On the altar animals were sacrificed.

Moses took the blood from the sacrifices. Half of it he sprinkled on the altar as if he were giving it to God. Then he read out the rules very slowly and carefully.

'Will you accept these commands?' asked Moses. 'Will you obey God?'

The people all replied, 'Yes, we will accept these commands. We will obey God.'

'Then,' said Moses, 'I seal this agreement in blood. Here is the blood of the covenant.'

As he said this, he went among the people and sprinkled the rest of the blood on them. 'A covenant that is sealed in blood cannot be broken,' said Moses.

ABOUT THE STORY

The setting for this story is Sinai, where Moses experienced his call through the burning-bush vision. Like Jacob's experience at Bethel that event had already made the place sacred. Moses wanted the people to feel the presence he had felt.

The Ten Commandments are divided into two groups. The first four are concerned with obligations to God, the last six obligations to one's fellow human beings. However, obligations to one's fellows stem from obligations to God and adherence to the will of God is shown and judged through attitudes to humans.

The wording is almost entirely negative. The Commandments are rules about what not to do. Nevertheless, for the period, they represent a very advanced moral code. Kipling's immortal line 'there ain't no Ten Commandments east of Suez' should serve to remind us, in our Western arrogance, that, in fact, they came from east of Suez. It might also cause us to reflect on what sort of social and moral codes existed in Britain some 3200 years ago!

The Book of Exodus gives more than one account of the giving of the Law. (See Exodus 20 for the most commonly used narrative.) This older version, connected with the idea of a blood oath, has been chosen because of its symbolism – a symbolism that is often more connected with childhood pledges of the 'cut my throat and hope to die' type than with the more sophisticated world of most adults, although it persists in movements like Freemasonry.

'Covenant' means an agreement and/or a testament. This agreement is between God and the people, made on their behalf by Moses. (The word 'Israel' here means 'the people of God'.)

IDEAS FOR EXPLORING FURTHER

Rules   Why did the Israelites need rules? Discuss why there are school rules. Can pupils suggest amendments/devise class rules? Write the Commandments on separate cards. Work in groups to rank them in levels of importance, drawing out the values/reasons for decisions. Separate the first four (duties to God) from the last six (duties to other people). With older pupils, discuss how far we need both. Compare the rules of religious traditions and faith communities. Try to explain similarities/differences between these.

Promises   Discuss experiences of promises made, kept or broken. Who makes promises, when and why? (E.g. New Year, godparents, confirmation, bar-mitzvah, weddings, law courts, religious vows.) Are some promises more important than others? Why? What symbols are used when making promises? (E.g. rings, swearing on the Bible, the five K's of Sikhs.) Why did Moses sign the Israelite agreement in blood? How do promises affect relationships?

15

A God in a Box in a Tent

Exodus 25: 1 – 30: 38

How will the people remember God when we leave the holy mountain? thought Moses. We can't take the mountain with us.

The answer came to him as he prayed to God. The Israelites must build a temple. In it they would keep all their sacred things. The stones from the mountain with the ten rules written on them would have to have a very special place.

The temple could not be made of stone or bricks. It would have to be a special tent. The Israelites called it a tabernacle. They would take it with them wherever they went. There would be plenty of time to build a great temple of stone when they finally settled down in one place.

Moses called all the people together. He told them what was wanted. 'Go to your tents,' he said, 'and bring out all your most precious things. Only the best is good enough for God. We are going to build a tabernacle where we will worship him. We will fill it with beautiful ornaments of gold and silver. The tabernacle itself will be made of goats' hair dyed purple and scarlet. We must also find beautiful wood and oil for lamps.'

The people went back to their tents. Most of them were happy to give everything they had. Others grumbled. They did not want to give up their gold necklaces and bracelets.

All the things were put together in heaps. Then the craftsmen went to work.

Cloth was woven and dyed and cut. Wood from the acacia tree' was cut and carved and polished. The gold objects were melted down over large fires. From the molten gold new ornaments were made. Even the rings which were to hold up the curtain walls of the tabernacle were made of pure gold.

While all this was going on to make the Tabernacle of God another object was also being made. It was a wooden chest about a metre and a half long. It too was carved from acacia wood. In each side gold rings were fixed. Poles were pushed through the rings. The whole box could then be lifted up and carried on the shoulders of walking men.

Into this chest were to be placed the most sacred items that the Israelites possessed. These were the stones from the mountain with God's commands written on them. This was the agreement which had been sealed in blood.

Wherever these stones went, it seemed as if God went too. In fact many people believed that God himself as good as lived in the box with the stones. Because it carried the most sacred objects it was called The Ark of the Covenant. The Ark was so sacred that no one was allowed to touch it. Everyone was prepared to die rather than see it taken by an enemy.

At last the Tabernacle and the Ark were finished. The time had come to leave the holy mountain. The long line of people once again set off across the desert.

At the front of the long column the Ark was carried by its long poles on the shoulders of the priests. It was as if God led the way.

The Tabernacle was carried in many separate parts. Whenever the people stopped, the parts would be brought together and the Tabernacle would be put up.

First, there was the courtyard, an open space surrounded by a fence. That was where the ordinary people gathered. Inside the main tent the priests would make sacrifices on behalf of all the people. But only one man was allowed to go into the most holy place of all.

That was the Holy of Holies. It was like a tent inside the main tent or Tabernacle. In the Holy of Holies was placed the

Ark of the Covenant. In the Ark lay the sacred stones. Only the High Priest was allowed to enter the Holy of Holies.

For many years the children of Israel were desert nomads. They wandered from place to place, sometimes stopping for a few weeks, sometimes for a few months. Whenever they stopped the Tabernacle was put up.

There came a time when the Israelites began to feel that they did not want to wander any more. Somewhere there was a promised land. Moses led them on but by now he was a very old man.

NOTES

ABOUT THE STORY

Moses had met with God at Sinai, first during the burning-bush incident and secondly at the giving of the Ten Commandments. Now he and the Israelites wanted to take this God with them to the Promised Land. Their concept was of a God who was especially to be found in this one place but who could be transported through objects identified with that place.

At this stage the Israelites were nomads who yearned to settle down. They needed a temple, not only to worship God in but also to house him. For the meantime, however, he, like they, must live in a tent. Nevertheless, it would have to be a special tent, the best that could be produced despite the people's state of deprivation. All the jewellery and special items that they were able to salvage in the flight from Egypt must be sacrificed for the task.

The most sacred objects were the tablets of stone cut from Sinai rock and bearing the Commandments. These were to be kept within the most precious item of furniture, the Ark, or, to give it its full title, deriving from its sacred contents, the Ark of the Covenant. In transit it would be conveyed only by those specially set aside for that task. They must defend it with their lives. When not in transit it would be placed in the inner sanctuary, the Holy of Holies, to which only the High Priest would have access.

We have in this story the developing idea of sacred place and a sacred priesthood. The power of God may emanate from one place but the Israelites can carry it with them. In part this means taking a bit of the mountain (the tablets of stone) with them. From this point onwards the search is on for a permanent holy place where the Ark can finally be brought to rest. Then God will have been transported from Sinai to a new location, as yet unknown, which, in turn, will become just as sacred.

IDEAS FOR EXPLORING FURTHER

Valued Possessions   Invite children to talk about their special possessions. What are their most precious possessions and why? Does their worth have anything to do with monetary value? If the children had to leave home in a hurry with one small case, what would they take with them? Do they bring home stones from a holiday beach or mountain? Why? Working in small groups, ask children to draw their most treasured possession. Let the group members relate the 'virtues' of their treasure and then discuss whether they would swop it for someone else's. Share experiences with the whole class. Make a list of reasons why something may be special. Write prose or a poem to express feelings when faced with swopping.

Holy Possessions   Discuss artefacts which are considered to be sacred or special within different religious traditions. Collect/make pictures of artefacts and label to show similarities/differences. If appropriate, use real artefacts, but sensitive handling is essential. It may be better to invite people to talk about what certain artefacts mean to them, or to look at artefacts *in situ* in a religious building. (NB   Nowadays, the Ark in a synagogue is usually a cupboard, not a box, and contains the fuller Law – the Torah. However, the Ten Commandments will be written above the doors.) Discuss especially holy places within religious buildings.

16

Rahab and the Spies

Joshua 2

After many years of wandering in the desert the Israelites came to the edge of the Jordan valley. From the high mountains of Moab they could look down on the river. On the other bank stood Jericho – the City of Palm Trees.

Moses looked down at it all. God spoke to him.

'This is the land I promised your people,' said God. 'At last you can see it. But your work is done. You will not cross the river.'

There Moses died. He was buried in the mountains of Moab. His place as leader was taken by Joshua.

Joshua called two men to him. 'Go across the river and spy out the land,' he said. 'Go into Jericho city and see how strong the walls are. Don't get caught.'

That night the two men set off. They waded across the river. Next day when the gates were open they walked into Jericho looking like merchants.

They walked around the city walls. Some poor people had their houses there. One woman, called Rahab, invited them in. Her house was built into the city wall. It had a window in the city wall itself.

Suddenly outside in the street there was shouting. Rahab went out to see what it was all about. A minute later she came running back indoors. 'Quick,' she said. 'You must hide.'

'What for?' cried the two Israelites.

'They are looking for you. They think you are Israelite spies. They are right, aren't they?'

Rahab did not wait for an answer. She made the two men lie down on the roof where she had some flax drying out. She covered them with the stalks of flax. There was a hammering at the door. She ran to open it.

'Where are they?' demanded the soldiers.

'Where are who?' asked Rahab.

'The two men who came here,' was the answer. 'They were spies of the Israelites.'

'Oh,' gasped Rahab, 'I did not know. They left a little while ago. They went that way.'

She pointed through the window towards the River Jordan and the Israelite camp away in the distance on the other side.

'If you go quickly,' Rahab added, 'you may catch them.'

Up on the roof the two men could hear everything. They held their breath, hardly daring to move. They gave a great sigh of relief as they heard a soldier say, 'Come on. Let's get after them.' There was a noise of men running, then silence.

A few minutes later Rahab pulled away the flax and they sat up.

'Why are you doing this for us?' asked one of the men.

'Because I have heard about your God,' said Rahab. 'We know all about your escape from Egypt. Everyone here knows that you will win any battle.'

That night Rahab tied some sheets together to make a rope. She hung it from her window. The two spies got ready to climb down it. Before they did so, one of them turned to Rahab. 'When we come,' he said, 'hang a piece of red cloth at this window. Make sure every member of your family is inside this house. Then they will not be harmed.'

With that they slid down the rope and vanished into the night. They made their way back to Joshua.

71

ABOUT THE STORY

This story has been selected as little more than a link between the Mosaic tradition and the settlement in Canaan. We have jumped the prolonged wandering in the wilderness to the point at which the Promised Land is sighted. With the destination in view Moses dies, to be succeeded by Joshua. Does this seem unjust? That depends on how individualistic we are. It has been said that 'the religious person is one who sees his or her life as part of a much greater whole, a larger story of which their lives are but a tiny part'. Concentration simply on our own life span would seem to be one of the by-products of modern secularism. Moses is a leader of gigantic stature but what matters is not the individual. It is the 'people of God'. Joshua appears much more as a straightforward military leader although with a direct, simple faith, like many generals.

The story of Rahab seems lacking in any great moral or religious depth. She was probably a prostitute, redeemed here by her prompt action in saving the two spies. One must imagine a small, isolated city suddenly plunged into a state of feverish excitement and activity by the emergence out of the desert across the river of an alien horde, apparently intent on conquest.

The fact that Rahab's dwelling is within the thickness of the city wall itself would explain the spies' interest. It is the wall which is to collapse in the following story. We might assume that the state of the wall and its defences would have been the main concern of their mission. Jericho's strategic position is as a crossing-point of the Jordan, the gateway into Palestine. It remains to this day the major crossing-point between East Jordan and its West Bank, now occupied by Israel.

IDEAS FOR EXPLORING FURTHER

Oral Communication   Discuss how Rahab would have heard about Israel's God. Who would have brought news of events in Egypt? What was the importance of the spoken word in a world without books, TV, radio? Talk about the value of oral tradition in many cultures and how some people are trained to repeat stories and scriptures word for word (e.g. the Qur'an).

Truth   How would Rahab have judged the truth of what various people said about Israel? In what ways do people experience events differently and select what to relate in light of personal preferences? Ask pupils to think back to an event shared recently. Invite individuals or small groups to write down key words, or to make an audio tape of their recollections. With younger/less-able children interview groups and help them to record their thoughts. Make comparisons and seek reasons for different recollections. Refer to varying newspaper accounts of particular events. Collect head-lines or articles to compare. Discuss the complexity of singling out the truth in what is said/written. (NC *History*: AT 2)

17

And the Walls Came Tumbling Down

Joshua 6: 1–23

The men of Jericho stood on the city walls. They waited with fear. Below them were the tents of the Israelites. The men of Israel were forming up. Soon the battle must begin. The city gates were shut and barred. Would the Israelites attack the gates or try to get in over other parts of the wall?

'What's that at the front of the column?' said one soldier to another. 'It looks like a box on two poles.'

'It is,' replied the other. 'They call it the Ark of the Covenant. It is said they keep their God in it.'

'Do you believe that?' asked the first soldier.

His friend laughed. 'He would have to be a pretty small God to be kept in there,' he said. 'But all the same it makes our people nervous. There is no doubt from what I've heard that every Israelite will die for that box and what is in it. It's got something to do with their God and He seems all-powerful. Look. What are they doing now? Where are they going?'

He pointed to the Israelites. They had been marching straight towards the city gates. But now they had turned and were marching alongside the city walls just outside the range of stones or arrows.

The soldiers of Jericho started to jeer and shout. There was no answer. On and on the Israelites marched. At the front were seven priests blowing on rams' horns. Apart from that there was total silence. Behind the priests came the Ark of the Covenant. Then came Joshua and all the men of Israel. Nobody spoke. There was no noise except for the tramp of feet, the seven rams' horns, and the shouts of the men of Jericho. Even these died away. They were ready for a fight. They did not know what to make of this strange, silent march.

The Israelites went right round the city wall until they came back to the city gate.

'This is it,' said the soldier. 'Get ready. They will attack now.'

But he was wrong. When the Israelites came back to where they had started, they turned and went back to their camps.

'What do you make of that?' asked the soldier.

'I don't know,' came the reply, 'but it makes me more nervous than fighting.'

Next day the same thing happened again – and the next day, and so it went on for a week.

On the seventh day the soldiers of Jericho were on the wall as usual. 'Here we go again,' they said to one another. The silent column began to march round the city. On and on went the weird noise of the rams' horns, like bagpipes.

'That noise drives me crazy. I even hear it in my sleep,' said one soldier.

As the Israelites came back towards the gate, the men of Jericho got ready to stand down.

'No, wait,' called an urgent voice. 'Something's happening.'

Sure enough, the Israelites had not gone back to camp as they usually did. They kept marching. The silent column went round the city again and then again.

They were going round for the seventh time. It had been a long day. All the time there had been no noise except the tramp, tramp, tramp of marching and the constant wail of the horns. Suddenly even that stopped. There was total silence. By this time the men of Jericho were very nervous.

Without warning the silence was shattered. The seven priests at the front of the march raised their rams' horns to their mouths again. The seven trumpet notes blared out into the silence, louder than ever. The reply was immediate. Every man of Israel shouted and yelled. The noise was deafening. It went on and on.

The men of Jericho at last found their voices. They began to shout back. Suddenly their shouts turned to cries of panic. Beneath their feet the city wall began to shake and tremble. Cracks began to appear, small at first, then larger. In places stones and rocks in the wall began to fall out. There was panic. The walls of Jericho came tumbling down.

The men of Israel rushed in. No one could stop them. The city was captured without any real battle.

From one small window, in a part of the city wall which was still standing, fluttered a piece of red cloth. It was the house of Rahab. Inside she sat with all her family, feeling very frightened. All of them were rescued.

NOTES

ABOUT THE STORY

The Book of Joshua is the first of six books (the others are Judges, 1 and 2 Samuel, 1 and 2 Kings) which record the history of the Israelites from their entry into the Promised Land until the Exile, when they were forcibly removed some six hundred years later. This is not detached history. It is sacred history. The conviction throughout is that God is in control and events are the working-out of his purpose.

In incidents such as this one, when the Israelites emerge triumphant, that purpose seems easy to recognize. It is, however, to the lasting credit of these ancient chroniclers that they remained consistent and attempted to show God's purpose in Israel's failures as well as her successes.

In the biblical version this story of the capture of Jericho is told through the eyes of the captors. This book reverses the perspective by telling the story from the vantage point of the defenders on the battlements. It is fear of the God of the attackers which haunts these defenders rather than fear of the invaders themselves. The prominence of the Ark at the front of the procession, the priests, the recurring ceremonial, the tight, spine-chilling self-control are all aspects which this retelling attempts to convey.

Explanations of exactly how the walls collapsed are necessarily limited. There is strong archaeological evidence to suggest that there was a major destruction at this period. The walls of Jericho have been built and rebuilt many times. What mattered for the Israelites was not how, but simply the fact that they triumphed easily.

75

What has been omitted from this retelling is the biblical ending, in which every living thing in Jericho, except Rahab and her family, is put to death. If it is thought necessary to add this then it should be borne in mind that the attitude of the time was that of eliminating evil rather than of deliberately destroying human beings, in exactly the same way as we today would try to destroy foot-and-mouth disease by slaughtering a whole herd of cattle. It was seen as a conflict between the holy and the unholy, the sacred and the profane. It would be comforting to think we had totally lost that state of mind today but twentieth-century history is surely against such a conclusion.

IDEAS FOR EXPLORING FURTHER

Cooperation   Would Joshua have had the same effect on the people of Jericho if he had walked around the walls alone? Why was it important that everyone went? Discuss times when cooperation and teamwork are vital for a successful outcome or the well-being of everyone. Compare human efforts to the working parts of any machine and draw out that on its own each part has little value, whereas the whole machine achieves an important purpose. Ask pupils to think of something they could achieve by working together which they couldn't achieve alone. Help older pupils to list the emotions which might have been felt within the walls over a week (e.g. fear, curiosity, irritation, foreboding, anger, uncertainty, concern about food and water stocks).

Ritual   What rituals do children have? (E.g. getting up, coming to school, in school, returning home, at weekends, etc.) Why have rituals? What feelings do they create? (E.g. security, a sense of belonging, of demarcation of time, of some activities being more important than others, of a need to be reflective.) What about religious rituals? Are symbols used? What thoughts and feelings do these rituals convey? Can we be frightened by rituals we do not understand? Draw on children's experience with regard to learning about how people from other traditions worship, cook, greet each other, etc. What seems strange and why?

18

Gideon's Three Hundred

Judges 6: 11–16; 7: 1–9, 19–21

The galloping camels thundered across the valley.

'Run, the Midianites are coming,' went up the cry.

Everybody ran for safety.

It happened time and time again. Nothing could move faster than a galloping camel. The Midianites were raiders. They came quickly, robbed the farms and villages and galloped away.

At Ophrah in the Jezreel valley a young man called Gideon was threshing wheat. He was doing it indoors so that he would not be seen by any raiders. He could not throw the wheat in the air, which was the easy way. He had to beat it, one sheaf at a time. It was hard work.

Suddenly he heard a voice. It came from outside. 'God is with you, you brave hero,' it said.

Gideon looked round. There under an oak tree sat a man he had never seen before. Gideon put down the threshing-stick and went outside. 'If God is on our side,' he said to the stranger, 'why does all this raiding go on?'

'Because no one does anything about it,' came the reply. 'You're a strong man. You go and free your people from the Midianites.'

'Me?' exclaimed Gideon. 'Me? I come from one of the poorest families of our whole tribe, and I am the youngest person in the family. What can I do about it?'

'God is with you,' came the answer. 'He can do anything if you will let Him use you.'

Gideon went on arguing but in the end he took up the challenge.

He went out and about and got men to follow him. The Midianites heard about him and arrived with thousands of men. The Israelites got ready to meet them.

God spoke to Gideon. 'You have got too many men,' He said.

'But the Midianites have already got more than us,' said Gideon.

'Never mind,' said God. 'Tell your men that if anyone is frightened he can go home.'

Gideon did so, and thousands of his followers went off.

'Still too many,' said God. 'Take them down to the water. Watch how they drink.'

Gideon did as he was told. He stopped his army by the river and told the men to drink.

Some quickly ran down to the water's edge and lay on their stomachs, or got down on their knees, drinking like dogs. Just a few looked round, made a cup with their hands and drank standing up, ready for anything.

'Take those,' said God. 'Send the rest home.'

Gideon was left with just three hundred men.

That night God spoke to Gideon again. He said, 'Get up and go down to the Midianite camp. It is all yours.'

Gideon divided his men up into three groups – a hundred in each group. Every man carried a sword, a trumpet and a pot with a candle inside. At the edge of the camp they stopped. No one had heard them. The Midianites were expecting a huge army.

Inside the camp all seemed quiet. The sentries were half asleep. It was the middle of the night. Suddenly, close by, the silence was broken by a loud trumpet blast. It was followed by a great crashing noise.

Gideon's men has thrown their candle-pots on to the ground. To the Midianites it seemed as if suddenly hundreds of lights had appeared from nowhere.

Then three hundred trumpet blasts filled the air. A great

shout broke through the night. 'For God and for Gideon,' shouted the three hundred together. 'For God and for Gideon.'

There was panic. The Midianites could not get out of their tents fast enough. They thought there were thousands and thousands of Israelites attacking them. The lucky ones leapt on to camels and galloped off into the darkness. Others just ran. Gideon's men chased after them still shouting 'For God and for Gideon'.

Gideon went back home. He broke down all the altars which had been set up to other gods. He made sure that the only God who was being worshipped was Israel's God.

NOTES

ABOUT THE STORY

This and the following story from the Book of Judges can present a number of problems but these need not detract from telling them as straightforward 'hero tales', which is how most Jewish children will receive them.

The period of the Judges is a cloudy period in Israel's history. It forms a link between the momentous Exodus narratives and the emergence of a settled state. Despite the total conquest of Jericho it would be wrong to see the occupation of the land as akin to a modern invasion in which one nation state is taken over by another. The tribes of Israel appear to have established a central shrine at Shiloh but, apart from that and the conquest of the really key strategic city of Jericho, this period saw them settling in amongst the Canaanite inhabitants and beginning to adapt to their agricultural way of life all too readily.

With the changeover to agriculture a new spiritual danger emerged. The Canaanite gods were fertility gods. Every settlement possessed a shrine to the local Baal (plural 'Baalim'). To many Israelites it seemed that their own God was a desert deity. What would he know of crops and farming? The temptation to switch allegiance was very great.

In addition there was no longer one central figure approaching the stature of Moses or even Joshua. Leadership was local rather than national. It took the form of 'judges'. In Hebrew the word originally referred to someone who read the oracles. By this period a judge had become what we might term a chieftain. He would be the arbiter in dispensing community justice. That would be bound up with religious belief and practice but he would equally exercise some civil and military leadership. Something between a medieval lord of the manor and a nineteenth-century Wild West sheriff, he would gather together an armed force or posse if and when the need arose. Comparisons with the settlement of the American Mid-West are probably not altogether inappropriate for background atmosphere. Nor did such a context wholly exclude women. At least one – Deborah – is numbered among the Judges.

The Israelites were not the only group attempting to settle in Palestine. As the meeting-place of three continents it has always funnelled more than its fair share of human traffic. The Midianites were seen by the Israelites as marauders who could quickly destroy their fragile settlements.

This particular story of Gideon is set against the background of the combined threats of the Baalim and the Midianites. There is an immediate physical danger but at root there is a deeper spiritual one. It is Israel's God who must defeat the Midianites as a way of demonstrating his continuing presence and power. Only the truly faithful can fight the battle and the numerical disadvantage emphasizes God's compensating strength.

A variety of interpretations have been offered of this story and all may be valid. A small, highly disciplined force operating under cover of surprise may well have caused chaos among a much larger but disorganized group. The emphasis on imagination and native wit outsmarting brute strength and ignorance is also present once again. But where does the inspiration come from? For Gideon and subsequent Jewish historians there is no doubt. It comes from God. It is the God of Israel who emerges triumphant and whose power continues to hold sway.

IDEAS FOR EXPLORING FURTHER

Stereotyping Discuss pupil attitudes towards Midianites and Israelites. Do prejudices surface? Why? Do we assume things about people we hardly know? Make links with Europeans and native peoples of North America, attitudes to immigrants, refugees, etc. Note that minority groups are not always politically or socially inferior (e.g. Boers and British in South Africa, the British in India). Is any race wholly good/ bad, or is there good and bad in everyone and every nation? Consider the role of the media in presenting images about people/nations. Mount thought-provoking pictures on large sheets of paper. Cover with acetate. Use arrows to highlight areas of interest. Round the image, ask/write questions and indicate further information required before being able to give a fairer opinion about what is portrayed.

Partners with God Discuss the value of taking responsibility for putting things right, not just relying on other people. Would God want to use our hands and feet for action? What do religious traditions say about how we can listen to God, and be guided by him? How do we listen to God speaking in our inner selves? Let pupils identify factors which spoil their school environment, e.g. areas with litter, uninteresting school gardens, unexciting playground, bare walls, untidy cloakrooms. Can they take responsibility to improve matters in partnership with others? Pursue suggestions.

19

Samson and Delilah

Judges 16: 4–30

The Israelites used to love to hear stories of their heroes.
During the time when they were settling down in Canaan
their nearest rivals were the Philistines. Sometimes Israelites
and Philistines were quite friendly. At other times they were
fierce enemies.

Samson was one of the great heroes of the Israelites. He was
thought to be very, very strong but he wasn't always very
bright. Many people think that the stories about him are a bit
made up in places. It doesn't really matter whether they are
or not. The Israelites used to tell these stories around their
camp-fires. They enjoyed them and that made them feel good.
While the Philistines might have got the better of the
Israelites at times, the Israelites knew that with their belief
in God, they, like Samson, were bound to win in the end,
whatever the cost.

Samson fell in love with Delilah. Delilah was friendly with
the Philistines.

'Find out what makes him so strong,' the Philistine chiefs
said to her.

Delilah waited for Samson to come and see her. She ran her
hands over his thick, hairy arms and said, 'You are so strong. I
wonder what it would need to tie you down.'

Samson laughed. 'Try seven bowstrings,' he said.

Delilah got seven new bowstrings. Samson held out his hands and she bound them as tight as she could.

Just as she finished the last knot she looked out of the window. 'Help! The Philistines are coming,' she screamed.

With one pull of his hands Samson snapped the bowstrings like pieces of cotton.

Delilah tried again. This time Samson told her to use new rope. The same thing happened again. It snapped with one pull.

'You're just playing with me,' said Delilah sulkily. She made eyes at him. 'Come on, tell me. What really is too strong for you?'

Samson looked at her. She really was very attractive.

'It's my hair,' he said. 'If you were to weave that into your loom there is no way in which I could escape from that.'

Delilah made him lie down. Then she took his long black hair and wove it into her large wooden loom. He seemed completely tied down. Surely no one could get out of that. She looked up. 'The Philistines, the Philistines!' she shouted.

Behind her there was a terrible noise of splintering wood. She whirled round. Samson had jumped to his feet. The loom was smashed to pieces. Bits of it hung from Samson's hair.

Delilah sulked even more. 'You don't love me at all,' she said, nearly crying. 'If you did, you would trust me. You're laughing at me. You're always laughing at me.' She burst into tears.

Samson put his arm round her. 'All right, all right,' he said. 'Don't cry. I'll tell you. It is my hair. My strength is there. It doesn't matter what you do with my hair as long as you don't cut it off. If you did that I just wouldn't be strong any more, even if I wasn't tied up.'

Delilah looked at him. This time she was sure he was telling the truth. When he had gone she went out and told the Philistine chiefs what he had said.

A few days later Samson was at Delilah's house again. He fell asleep on the bed. Delilah tiptoed out of the house. She came back with one of the Philistines. Very carefully they cut Samson's hair. Then they woke him up. Samson was helpless. Other Philistines came in. Samson was overpowered and taken away.

The Philistines were cruel to Samson. They put out his eyes and blinded him. When his hair grew again and his strength came back they made him work at the grinding mill. It was a job normally done by oxen or camels.

A great day of festival came. The Philistines were going to worship their god, called Dagon. They took the blind Samson along to show him off to the rest of the people. He was chained to a stone pillar.

The temple of Dagon was held up by two great stone pillars, a bit like a large circus tent except that it was made of stone.

The ceremony went on. Nobody took any notice of Samson. Suddenly there was a creaking noise. People looked round and screamed.

Samson was pushing with all his might against both pillars. He called out a prayer. 'O God of Israel,' he shouted at the top of his voice, 'give me back my strength, just this once.'

He leaned with all his weight and strength into the pillars. They bent and then cracked. People screamed and tried to run. They knocked one another over. Bits of the roof began to fall. Then there was a terrible rumbling noise. The whole roof and the walls fell in. All the Philistine chiefs were killed. So was Samson. The temple of Dagon was completely destroyed.

ABOUT THE STORY

The story of Gideon was set against the challenge from the Midianites. That of Samson is set in the context of the much greater threat of the Philistines. It is in the Book of Judges that we first hear of them but their history is interwoven with that of the Israelites for five or six centuries. So powerful was their influence that the name which they gave to this area of the world, Palestine, is still in use today.

The Philistines had come from the Greek islands, predominantly from Crete, and remained a trading and seafaring people. Their arrival coincided with the discovery of iron and they would appear to have known the secret of smelting, which gave them a huge advantage in terms of both agriculture and weaponry.

Again we are aware that there was intermingling, not unlike the present-day mixture of Arabs and Jews. Indeed, what is now known as the Gaza Strip roughly formed the bridgehead of the early Philistine settlement. It consisted of the five cities of Gaza, Ashkelon, Ashdod, Ekron and Gath, each ruled by a different 'Lord of the Philistines' but, as a group, capable of fast, united action. By contrast Israel remained a loose confederation of tribes held together by the idea of covenant, symbolized by the Ark kept at Shiloh.

Against all these supposed disadvantages one man with a combination of native wit and sheer physical prowess wreaks havoc and shows the power of Israel's God. Apart from the final incident in his life Samson does not come across as a very edifying figure but his earlier wild life-style is more than cancelled out by this one great sacrifice. In all Western cultures he has passed into legend as a folk-hero, his name synonymous with physical strength (e.g. Milton's 'Impotence of mind in body strong').

IDEAS FOR EXPLORING FURTHER

Strength   Think of people the children respect and admire greatly and make a list of their qualities. Does strength figure on the list? How important is physical strength? How should it be used? What does it mean to have a strong character? Identify people who do/did not give in to evil easily, who persevere(d) in time of trouble, etc. Contrast with Story 20.

In small groups, use different materials to make walls or pillars. Design a fair test to find out which is the most difficult to break. (NC *Science*: types and uses of materials; forces)

84

20

The Call of Samuel

1 Samuel 3: 1–19

The Israelites had settled down. No longer did they move from place to place like desert nomads. They built themselves houses and, instead of only herding sheep and goats, they started to make farms as well.

Back in the desert their grandparents and great grandparents had said that when they settled down the first thing they would do would be to build a great temple. They had forgotten. The present Israelites were too busy on their farms. Only at Shiloh was there a real temple, where the sacred Ark was kept. And fewer and fewer people bothered about it.

The old priest who looked after the temple was a man called Eli. He was getting very old and he was worried. Who was going to take his place when he died? Nobody seemed to care any more. His sons were not at all interested. Just as Moses had feared, a lot of people seemed to think that God had been left behind in the desert. They did not seem to need him any more.

Eli felt very tired. There were times when he wondered himself whether God was really there. He was not a very good priest and he knew it. But was he the last?

There was a noise outside. Someone was coming. The old priest got up and went outside. A woman stood there with a young boy, about seven years old. Her name was Hannah. Eli had met her before. She had once come to him to ask for a blessing because she had no children. Now she had five. Samuel was her eldest. She had brought him to work at the temple. It was her way of giving thanks to God.

Samuel liked the work, and Eli was glad to have him, but he did not solve the problem. Samuel cleaned the temple and helped get it ready for services but he was not a priest. Eli was going blind as well as getting old. Several years went by and nothing happened. He could not go on much longer.

Then one night Samuel suddenly woke up. He sat up in bed and listened. Not a sound. Somebody had called. That was what had wakened him. It must have been Eli. There was no one else about. The night was very still. Samuel threw back the goatskin blanket and got up. He crept into the room where Eli slept. 'Yes, what is it?' he asked.

Eli was surprised to see him. 'I haven't called you,' he said. 'Go back to bed.'

Samuel went back to bed. He fell fast asleep. Suddenly he was wide awake again. There was no doubt about it this time. The voice was still ringing in his ears. 'Samuel, Samuel,' it called. He leapt out of bed and ran to Eli's room.

'Yes, master –' he began.

But Eli interrupted him. 'No. No, my son, I have not called you. Go back to bed again.'

The third time it happened it was even clearer. Samuel went straight to Eli's bedside and said, 'I did hear a voice. You were calling me.'

Eli was quiet. Could it really be happening? No one had had this sort of vision of God for many, many years. Eli himself had just gone on from day to day, but he had heard and read about these things. Perhaps something exciting was about to happen. He turned to Samuel. 'Go back to bed,' he said. 'But if the voice comes to you again, don't run in here. Stay where you are and simply say "Speak, Lord, your servant is listening".'

Samuel did as he was told although he did not understand it.

Sure enough the voice came again. 'Samuel, Samuel,' it called.

The boy trembled but he lay still and said the words Eli had told him to say: 'Speak, Lord, your servant is listening.'

The message came to him clear and certain. He was to

become the priest in place of Eli. Samuel lay awake until morning.

At daybreak he got up and began to get the temple ready for the day.

Eli came in. 'What happened?' he asked.

Samuel said nothing.

'Tell me,' Eli said again. 'Tell me what happened in the night.'

Still Samuel hesitated. How could he tell the old man that his time was finished and that he must hand over his work?

Eli saw what was going on in Samuel's mind. 'Come on,' he said. 'Tell me everything. I want to know the truth.'

So Samuel told Eli of the vision he had had. He gave him all the details. When he had finished he expected Eli to be very angry. But Eli simply nodded. 'You have done right to tell me,' he said. 'It was the voice of God which you heard.'

Within a short time Eli died, but before that he had made sure that all the people knew that Samuel had been chosen to follow him. Samuel was to be the new priest and the spokesman for God in Israel.

NOTES

ABOUT THE STORY

Behind this simple story the continued menace of the Philistines lurks ominously. The faith, which was all that held Israel together, was crumbling away. Nowhere was this more visible than at Shiloh, where no one could be found to take on the succession of guarding the sacred Ark, the symbol of all that Israel stood for.

As the faith began to die so inevitably the sense of community dissipated. The real crisis point comes in the biblical chapter immediately following this account of the call of Samuel (1 Samuel 4). Israel suffers a military defeat at the hands of the Philistines and when, in a last desperate attempt to reverse their fortunes, a group brings the Ark from Shiloh to the field of battle the worst imaginable scenario occurs. The Ark itself is captured and taken off by the triumphant Philistines. Not only the Israelites but also their God has been defeated. News of this disaster, together with the knowledge that his two sons have died in the battle, causes the collapse and death of Eli.

It was against this background that Samuel took over as guardian of the shrine. It is hardly surprising, therefore, that he should have become such a revered figure for later generations.

This story from his boyhood shows the basis of his later reputation. In stark contrast with Samson, Samuel's authority from the beginning was wholly spiritual, rather than physical or even political. He was to become acknowledged as a seer, a person with direct intuitive insight, whose experience of God was direct. His sacrifice was in life-long service to the community, motivated by his inner convictions of God.

IDEAS FOR EXPLORING FURTHER

Prayer   Discuss how prayer can be listening as well as talking to God. Consider the Quakers and the need for quiet. Talk about how the prayer positions of different religions help people to avoid distractions or show reverence. What makes a good place to pray? Does it have to be in a religious building? Let pairs of children have a variety of materials and a cardboard box in which to design and make a model of the kind of place in which people might like to pray. (NC *Technology; Science:* types and uses of materials)

Symbols   The Ark and temple were symbols of community. Discuss the role of flags, team colours, religious artefacts and buildings, emblems and logos. Let individuals or small groups design an emblem/logo for the class/school. Explore different techniques through art. Constructively discuss finished products. Analyse why people react positively to certain designs, colours, materials.

21

We Want a King

1 Samuel 8; 10: 17–24

'We want a king! We want a king!'

The crowd stood outside Samuel's house in the village of Ramah.

Samuel stood facing them. He was old now. His mind went back to the day, many years ago, when as a young boy he had replaced Eli. Now his turn had come. Like Eli's sons his own boys were not going to follow in his footsteps. All they thought about was money.

The elders had come a few days before. They had said to Samuel, 'Look, you are getting old. Your sons are not going to be like you. We don't want any of them as leaders. Other nations are led by kings. Why can't we have a king as well?'

'We've got a king,' Samuel had replied, 'the greatest king of all. God is our king.'

'We know that,' replied the elders. 'But we want an earthly king as well.'

Samuel got angry at this. Why couldn't his people understand? They were different. 'Think,' he said at last. 'Think what it will mean. If you have a king he will want to be rich. He will want a palace and a lot of servants. He will appoint all the generals and he will want the best of everything, the best fields, the best vineyards, the best cattle and so on. All this will have to be paid for. And you will have to pay for it with taxes.'

The elders had left but Samuel knew that he had not won.

Now the crowd had come. 'We want a king!' came the shout again.

Samuel felt very sad. All his life he had tried to show how the people of Israel could be led by God. They had not understood. Suddenly he felt God very close.

'Don't be saddened,' he heard God say. 'I should be the one to be sad. The people are not rejecting you. They are rejecting me. Go and make them a king. They will have to learn the lesson the hard way.'

Samuel went outside. He raised his hands. The crowd fell silent. 'God will find you an earthly king,' he said. 'Now go away. I shall call you together when I have news for you.'

The crowd cheered and went back to their homes.

A little while later Samuel sent out messengers to all parts of the country. All the tribes of Israel were to gather together at Mizpeh. They came in their hundreds and thousands. Some walked, some rode on donkeys. From every direction they came, and camped on the hillsides. To the north and east could be seen the mountains and the deserts of Palestine. To the west the green plains stretched down to the great sea. Away to the south the city of Jerusalem, with its white buildings, shone like a mirror on a hilltop.

When everybody was gathered together Samuel appeared at the top of the slope. He spoke to the crowd. 'This is what God says,' he thundered. 'I brought you out of Egypt. I have helped you in the promised land. I have done everything for you. Now you say "We want a king". You are weak. You don't have enough faith. But because you are weak I shall let you have your way. I shall give you a king.'

The crowd cheered. Samuel stepped down. The people knew what he was going to do.

Samuel took twelve stones. On each stone was marked the name of one of the twelve tribes. The crowd waited in silence. From which tribe would the king come? Samuel drew out his hand from the bag in which the stones had been placed. 'Your king,' he announced, 'will come from the tribe of Benjamin.'

There were murmurs. Benjamin was one of the smallest and weakest tribes.

'Now all the heads of the families of Benjamin come here,' called Samuel. A group of old men stepped forward. 'Each of you take a stone,' ordered Samuel. 'Write the name of your family upon it.'

The old men did as they were told. The stones were put in the sack.

Samuel stood in front of all the crowd again. He drew out his hand, looked at the stone and said, 'Your king shall come from the Matrite family.'

And now the really important moment had come. All the men of the Matrite family had come forward. Their names were placed on stones. As Samuel drew out a stone for the third time there was complete silence.

Samuel looked at the stone, looked up and proclaimed, 'Your king is Saul, the son of Kish.'

Everybody looked around. Who was he? Where was he? There was no movement. The men of the Matrite family looked anxious. They knew Saul but they could not see him. Where had he got to?

'He must be somewhere,' a voice called. 'Look among the donkeys and the baggage.'

They ran to where all the luggage was piled.

Saul was frightened. He was an ordinary man. How could he be the king of all Israel? That was why he had hidden himself. His brothers and cousins dragged him out. When they saw him the crowd broke into an excited murmur. Saul was enormous. He was head and shoulders taller than anyone else.

Samuel spoke: 'Behold, your king.'

The people cheered. 'Long live the king!' they shouted. 'Long live the king!'

But at the back of the crowd some men were already muttering angrily. Saul was honest and strong and a man of God. He was also a southerner. Some of the men who came from tribes in the north did not like the idea of being ruled by a man from the south.

91

ABOUT THE STORY

What is at stake here is the loss of an ideal, that of theocracy – direct rule by God – perhaps unique to the people of Israel in the ancient world and not common at any time. The later European model of the divine right of kings is the very thing which Samuel seeks to avoid in this incident. But his full advice is not taken. He may be recognized as a man of God but he nevertheless loses the argument to straight political considerations.

Samuel's description of what earthly kingship may mean can be seen as the prediction of a seer or as wisdom after the event, written in by the later chronicler (see Story 27).

What is not in doubt is that Saul was selected on criteria of Samuel's choosing. Much kingship throughout history has been based on a 'might is right' basis but although Saul appears to be chosen for his potential military ability his remit is strictly limited to the temporal. Spiritual leadership remains vested elsewhere and the kings would try to assume moral and religious leadership at their peril.

The need for a king was pragmatic: to unite the twelve tribes in resisting the Philistines. The Ark had been returned by them seven months after its capture because pestilence and plague had seemed to follow it everywhere, until no Philistine city would take it. Its status was thus enhanced but it was no longer seen as powerful enough to bring about military victory. A king was demanded because other, more successful nations had them.

Woven into the biblical account, but omitted in this retelling, is what many scholars take to be a quite separate, alternative story (see 1 Samuel 9: 1 – 10: 16).

IDEAS FOR EXPLORING FURTHER

Leadership   Discuss leadership in class: monitors, group leaders, team captains, etc. Why do we need them? Should one person always be leader? What abilities are required? (E.g. to listen, to serve, to remind, to act quickly, to judge fairly.) Should leaders be chosen for their talents? Consider some real-life or fictional leaders (men and women). Why are they admired or disliked? Ask pairs to draw an ideal leader. Put key words in/around the drawing or use them in a poem. Compare with Samuel and other known biblical leaders. Older pupils can consider why there are few female biblical leaders and discuss equal opportunities today.

National Leaders   Why were they chosen? (NC *History*: all CSUs; make links between the 'divine right of kings' and some British monarchs, e.g. CSU 2 – Tudor and Stuart times.) Discuss the powers of the British royal family today. Which are the most popular members and why? Talk with older children about hierarchies, looking at school, and the way shops, businesses, the police force, local and national government are organized. (NC *Citizenship*)

22

David the Musical Shepherd

1 Samuel 16: 16–23

David was a shepherd. He spent his life on the hills watching the sheep. They belonged to his father, Jesse. His life was hard. The hills were dry and rocky and there was not much grass. Wild animals were often about, especially at night, looking for a chance to attack the sheep.

The shepherd had to live with his sheep, sometimes for weeks at a time. He had to walk many miles looking for new pastures. At night he would lie down on the bare ground to sleep near the sheep. He had to be ready always to jump up and drive off hyenas and wolves, and perhaps even lions. He soon learned to use a spear, but David's favourite weapon was the sling. He carried it with him always. With it he could hurl a stone as fast and as straight as an arrow from a bow. There was plenty of time to practise.

A shepherd's life was a lonely one. Sometimes he would not see another human being for days at a time.

Like most shepherds, David felt very close to nature. He knew the mountains in all types of weather. At times he felt very small. It was then that he started to sing and to play. He made his own musical instruments. They were like small guitars. He made up his own songs as well. David was always singing.

Some of David's songs still exist. When he became famous some of them were written down. Today we can find them in the Bible, in the Book of Psalms.

Even when he was still a young boy, many people knew about David's gift for music. They talked about it and the news spread.

One day some men came to see David's father, Jesse. 'Saul the king is ill,' they said. 'He is in one of his black moods. They come upon him from time to time. Then he does nothing except sit in his chair all day. No one can talk to him.'

Jesse listened. 'That is sad,' he said. 'And it is bad for Israel. We need a king who can lead us properly. But why have you come to me? There is nothing I can do about it.'

'You have a son,' said the messengers.

'I have several,' replied Jesse. 'Which one are you talking about?'

'The one who sings and plays music. Music is the only thing which seems to help Saul when these moods come upon him. We have come to see if you will let your son come back with us.'

'But he is only a boy,' Jesse argued.

'That may be, but people talk about him far and wide.'

In the end Jesse agreed. David was fetched and he agreed to go away with the king's messengers.

It worked – at least for a while. Saul liked David, and David found a good friend in Saul's son Jonathan. David stayed with the king, and often when things were bad he would play and sing. He made up more and more songs.

Saul soon found that David was more than just a singer and a musician. He was also a good soldier. Although he was young, Saul made him his own personal armour bearer.

There was a lot of fighting to be done. The Israelites were being attacked from the south by the Philistines. The Philistines had come into Canaan from the sea. They were very strong and they had discovered the secret of making iron. The Israelites were still fighting with wooden spears and bronze swords and armour.

It looked as though the Israelites might lose. And then there was Goliath as well.

ABOUT THE STORY

Jewish historians, right down to our own day, have seen the reign of David as the Golden Age of Israel. The six-pointed star of David remains a central emblem of the modern State of Israel. Consequently there is much detail about David in the Jewish scriptures including an interest in his childhood.

If Saul was an unexpected choice for king because he came from an uninfluential tribe, David was equally surprising because he was the youngest of his family. It is Samuel who once again decides; there is no familial line of succession (see 1 Samuel 16: 1–16) and it is the household of Jesse which is chosen. However it is not the oldest son, Eliab, who is selected despite the normal assumptions of inheritance. As with Saul's selection Samuel's criteria for choice ignore convention and concentrate on the greater needs of the community of Israel.

We have here one of the rare accounts of childhood in the Bible although we must be careful not to think of that in very modern terms. Adolescence did not exist, any more than it did in Britain until the twentieth century. Youngsters moved directly from childhood to adulthood through some form of initiation but even quite young children might carry huge responsibilities. To take care of the flock was to have charge of the family's entire fortune.

Today there is renewed interest in the rhythm of nature and a religious interest in finding harmony with it, in contrast with the desire to fight and overcome it which has characterized so much Western Christianity in recent times. David is portrayed in this story as a child of the world in touch with the rhythms of the earth, its seasons and life in the wild. His songs reflect this. Not all the psalms ascribed to David are his but some almost certainly are. They are hugely neglected today.

IDEAS FOR EXPLORING FURTHER

God and Nature Look at creation stories in different traditions (e.g. *Worlds of Difference*, by E. Bisset and M. Palmer, World Wildlife Fund). How should people behave towards the environment? Which mysteries in the natural world cause some people to sense the hand of God? Let children recall and experience beautiful natural environments and have time to reflect and record their feelings. Consider the environment as a place of prayer (e.g. the role of trees for Buddhists).

Music and Song Explore links between music and feelings, and different responses to music. Do pupils play instruments or sing in choirs? Why? Discuss music we hear (e.g. pop, folk, classical, sacred). When and why do we use it? (E.g. assemblies, festivities, dance, ceremonies, films, TV.) Play pieces of music and ask for class reaction: why liked, what memories are evoked, etc. Emphasize variety of responses. Discuss criteria for, and draw up, a class 'Top Ten'. Create a slide/tape show, with pupils selecting slides of natural scenes and musical excerpts to accompany them. Discuss favourite religious songs. Find the 'Top Three' and use for assembly, explaining choices. Use songs from different languages to illustrate one theme. Discuss why some stories are told through music/opera (e.g. Prokofiev's 'Peter and the Wolf', Handel's 'Messiah', Lloyd Webber's 'Jesus Christ Superstar'). Help older pupils to compose music and words for songs, or to provide new words for known tunes. Explore how the Psalms (e.g. number 23) have been set to music. (NC *Science*: sound and music) See Chapter 23, 'Music's Contribution to Junior RE', in *The Junior RE Handbook*, edited by R. Jackson and D. Starkings.

Childhood   David had heavy responsibilities, guarding the sheep (the family fortune). Compare with childhood roles through the ages. (NC *History*: SSU on domestic life, families and childhood) Discuss rites of initiation to adulthood.

23

David and Goliath

1 Samuel 17

Goliath was a giant of a man. He was three metres tall, a real freak. He had a voice to go with his size. 'Come on and fight,' he bellowed across the valley.

On the other side stood Saul and the Israelites. They listened and they were frightened. They didn't know what to do.

'Come on,' shouted Goliath again. 'One against one. Who's going to come and fight? Send out your champion. If he can beat me, our army will surrender to you. If I beat him, you surrender to us. Nobody else will get killed.'

In the Israelite camp nobody moved. Even from this distance Goliath looked enormous. He stood half-way down the opposite hillside. His bronze helmet shone in the sun. It made him look even bigger. He wore armour too on his body and legs. The staff he carried looked like a tree trunk and he had a spear to match.

He must weight a ton, thought Saul. He could kill a normal man just by sitting on him.

'What's up?' came Goliath's voice again. 'Are you scared?'

From the ranks of the Philistines behind Goliath came a sound of distant laughter.

It was no good. If Saul sent a man, he would lose. If he didn't, his men would know he was scared. Saul didn't know what to do.

ind him he heard an argument taking place.

'What's going on?' said a voice Saul knew.

'Where did you come from?' asked another angry voice. 'Who's looking after the sheep this time?'

'The sheep are all right. Dad sent me with some things for you. What's going on?'

'Oh, nothing for kids like you. This is man's stuff.'

It was David arguing with his elder brother, Eliab. David had been back home on the farm. Eliab and his other brothers were part of Saul's army.

Just at that moment Goliath started shouting again. 'Come on,' he roared. 'Who's going to come and fight?'

David looked around. 'Well?' he asked. 'Who's going? What's that heathen Philistine got against the armies of God?'

'Oh, shut up, you cocky fool,' said Eliab, who had never liked David since he had been chosen to go to Saul. 'You've only come to see a fight.'

'What have I done now?' said David. 'All right,' he said. 'I'll go and fight him if you won't.'

Eliab laughed, but somebody had already told Saul that there was a volunteer.

Saul groaned when he saw who it was. 'You can't go,' he said to David. 'You're only a teenager. Goliath has been a soldier for years.'

'So what?' said David. 'I've taken on a lion and bears when I've been on my own with the sheep. He looks a bit like a bear,' he added, looking across to where Goliath stood.

For the first time Saul and his men smiled.

'All right,' said Saul. 'Get on with it and God be with you.' There was nothing else he could do. 'Take my armour,' he added. 'You will need it.'

Willing hands helped David put on Saul's heavy breastplate and helmet. Then the bronze leg-guards were strapped on. A sword was placed in one hand, a spear in the other.

David tried to walk. He couldn't. He stumbled and fell. It took four men to lift him up.

'Take this lot off,' gasped David. 'If I'm going to fight, I'll fight my way.'

Dressed only in a loincloth and carrying a sling, he set off down the hillside to the stream at the bottom.

Goliath saw him coming. He threw back his head and roared with laughter.

'Look at this,' he called out. 'They've sent out a little scrap for the birds.'

David had stopped at the stream. He bent down and chose five round stones. He put four in the bag he always carried round his neck. The other he put in his sling.

Goliath came down the hill. He walked heavily and he was still laughing.

David leapt across the stream and ran towards Goliath. 'It's you who's going to be food for the birds,' he called. 'The power I have is the strength of our God of Israel.'

Goliath still came on. David stopped. In his right hand he held his sling. He began to whirl it. Round and round it went, slowly and deliberately. Goliath thumped down the slope towards him.

He was ten metres away when, with a sudden hard twist of his arm, David let go of one of the sling straps. The stone flew out like a bullet.

Goliath had no chance. The stone caught him between the eyes. The ground shook as he fell. David moved like lightning. He grabbed Goliath's huge sword. It glinted in the sun as he raised it and then down it came. Goliath's head rolled slowly away from his body.

For a minute there was complete silence in the valley. Then there was a noise of running feet. David looked up. Behind him his own army was running down the hill shouting and cheering. Above him the Philistines were running in the opposite direction.

ABOUT THE STORY

Compressed within this well-known story there is the whole Davidic legend and much of the self-image of Israel too. The setting continues to be that of the Philistine menace and this incident marks the turning-point in Israel's struggle against that threat. It is a turning-point for David too, but the enhancing of his reputation is seen by the manic-depressive Saul as threatening his own status and position.

There is no justification for doubting a basic historical foundation for the story, even though details might have been exaggerated. At the same time it shows Israel's position in regard to her neighbours, or at least how she perceives it, then as now. Here with a vengeance is the small, apparently weak, God-fearing innocent threatened by, but taking on, the might of the well-armed, all-threatening giant and emerging victorious. David appears as something of a Charlie Chaplin or a Woody Allen figure as attempts are made to put Saul's armour on him. In the end he chooses his own methods, a classic example of guile over brawn.

The traditional image of David's armoury is of 'five little stones'. This might have been the case but even if he had failed with his first shots Goliath would still have had the problem of catching him. However, archaeological discoveries throughout Israelite encampments of this period show that sling-shots were often prepared stones, chipped into rough spheres somewhere between the size of a golf and a tennis ball. They would have been lethal when hurled from a sling.

IDEAS FOR EXPLORING FURTHER

Right over Might   Consider other stories which boost people's morale because good overcomes evil (e.g. Stories 43 and 44; wicked king Hiranya Kashyap and his good son Prahlad, see *Seasons of Splendour*, by Madhur Jaffrey; tales about the child Krishna, in the Mahabharata; Jack and the Beanstalk; Superman). Draw out similarities/differences concerning the role of people, their faith and the role of God.

Courage   Consider youngsters fighting cancer or handicap, or living in difficult conditions in Britain or abroad. (NC *Geography*: AT 2 – knowledge and understanding of places) How do they view the world? What are their hopes? How can they be helped to win their battles? If possible, visit a local children's ward. Think also of brave children during the Second World War (e.g. Jews in labour camps, Anne Frank, evacuees). Explore fiction (e.g. *Fireweed*, by Jill Paton Walsh; *Carrie's War*, by Nina Bawden). Discuss letters by Elizabeth I as a child, shut away by her sister, Mary I, and experiences of Victorian children. (NC *History*: CSU 2 – Tudor and Stuart times; CSU 3 – Victorian Britain; CSU 4 – Second World War; SSU on domestic life, families and childhood)

Faith in Action   Many people have undertaken daunting tasks, spurred on by inner conviction that this was what God wanted them to do (e.g. Helen Keller, Dr Barnardo). See the Faith in Action series, RMEP.

24

David Captures Jerusalem

2 Samuel 5: 6–10

Saul was dead. David was now king. For seven years he reigned from Hebron, the main city of his own tribe of Judah. He won many battles against the Philistines but there was one victory he wanted above all others. The city of Jerusalem had never been captured. It stood high on a hilltop. Its white walls shone in the sunlight.

David and his soldiers looked up towards it. The Jebusites who lived in the city looked down from the walls. They were laughing and jeering. Their voices travelled down the hillside.

'Go away,' they shouted. 'You won't get in here. We can defend this city with just our blind and a few cripples.'

It was true. David knew it. Long before he and his soldiers got up the steep slope to the bottom of the walls, they would be easy targets for arrows.

But he wanted Jerusalem. His own tribes from the south accepted him, but the northerners were not too happy. He had to have a capital city which did not belong to either group. Jerusalem was ideal. It could become the greatest city in all the world. But how could he capture it? His army had surrounded it for weeks. It seemed to make no difference.

He sat down and thought. Suddenly he sat up. Of course – water, the Jebusites had water. Where were they getting it from? If there was some sort of stream up inside the city walls it must come down into the valley. It must be an underground stream. If only.... David jumped to his feet. He must start looking.

101

They found it by a small pool in the Kidron valley. It was just a small hole in the rock with water trickling out. A man might squeeze into it – just. It would be wet and dark and dangerous. If they got stuck they would never get out again. David called his men together. He told them of his plan and asked for volunteers. A few men stepped forward.

That night when it was properly dark the soldiers went into the small tunnel, one behind the other. They had to squirm like snakes. The water running down was icy cold. It was pitch dark. In a few places the tunnel was quite wide. Most of the time it was like a narrow drain-pipe.

Outside, David and his men crept silently up the hill towards the main gate. They lay on the ground and waited. Hours went by. Nothing happened. The moon which had been high in the sky disappeared. It was very dark, but soon it would be dawn. There was no sound in the city except the occasional call of the sentries to one another. Then even that stopped.

Suddenly David sat up. What was that? Was he imagining things? No. There it was again. A soft creaking noise. David's men had heard it too. They all peered into the darkness. The creaking came again. It was the gate. Somebody had pulled back the bars and slowly the great gate was opening.

David got to his feet. He and his men drew their swords and began to run as quietly as possible up the hill. At any moment they expected to hear a sentry call and a trumpet sound the alarm. Nothing happened. The sentries over the gate all lay dead, attacked from behind as they looked out over the city wall.

There was little fighting. The Jebusites woke up to find David and the Israelites in control of the city.

Jerusalem was more than a capital city. It was a sacred place. It was here that Abraham had had a vision of God before the city was built, before David's ancestors had gone to Egypt and become slaves. It would be a sacred place again.

'The Ark must be brought to Jerusalem,' declared David. 'It will stay here for ever.'

ABOUT THE STORY

The five verses out of which this story has been fashioned are very obscure and it is probably impossible now to be specific about details. However, this should not blind us to the importance of this incident. What David achieved here was the reputation, first, for ingenuity and daring, and secondly, for fairness and justice.

In taking Jerusalem and making it his capital he showed that he favoured no one tribe, not even his own. For over seven years he had ruled from Hebron, the main city of his own southern tribe of Judah. It was something of a frontier town in the struggle against the Philistines but its choice still left the northern tribes suspicious and disgruntled. Comparison can be made with the choice in modern times of Washington D.C. and Canberra as neutral capitals.

Jerusalem is situated at a height of some 750 metres on top of a plateau, criss-crossed by steep ravines and valleys. It has always had water-supply problems and from this incident until the Roman period there were numerous initiatives to lay conduits. Nevertheless, it was the internal springs which made it basically able to withstand seige and as late as 1834, under seige by the fellahin, it was entered in the same way. It was an impregnable position and the taunts that it could be defended by the blind and lame had a ring of truth about them.

The mountain on which Jerusalem is built is traditionally the mountain to which Abraham brought Isaac. This association together with its neutrality made it an ideal substitute for Shiloh as the place to build the Temple and create a holy place. It was also, in time, to become the most holy place for Christians and the third most holy place, after Makkah and Medina, for Muslims. This story marks the start of that process of sanctification which persists down to the present day.

IDEAS FOR EXPLORING FURTHER

Jerusalem   Discuss how this city is sacred to Jews, Christians and Muslims. Link up with stories about religious events which took place here (e.g. Abraham and Isaac, Story 2; Jesus visiting the Temple as a child; Muhammad's lightning horse ride to the city). Compare holy places within Jerusalem: the Dome of the Rock mosque, the Wailing Wall, the Church of the Nativity. With older children, discuss current conflicting opinions about how Jerusalem should be used. (NC *Geography*: AT 4 – conflict over land use; also Story 29.) How far is modern tourism to Israel a kind of pilgrimage? What about places in Britain such as Walsingham, Lindisfarne, Iona? What about Amritsar, Benares, Kandy, Makkah? How can these places help people to develop their inner selves? What might they seek? Are people inspired by the history of a place and its spiritual meanings? Do they gain inner strength from these and become aware of new possibilities for the future?

103

25

Dancing in the Street

2 Samuel 6: 2–21

Jerusalem belonged to the Israelites. David made it his capital city. It stood on the highest hill. From its walls he could look out across his kingdom. In the far distance the River Jordan flowed along its deep valley. Beyond that lay the desert over which his forefathers had once travelled.

To the Israelites Jerusalem was even more than a capital city. It was a holy place. Before the walls had been built Abraham had walked on this hill. It was here that he had led Isaac to make a sacrifice.

David was determined to make Jerusalem a holy place again. The most sacred object of the Israelites must be brought into the city. Then they would have the biggest celebration that anyone could remember. Long, long ago Moses had dreamed of the day when all the wandering should stop. Now that day had arrived. David knew what had to be done.

'The Ark of the Covenant must be carried into Jerusalem,' he declared. 'This will be its final resting-place. It shall stay here for ever.'

The Ark was standing in a barn, covered in dust, almost forgotten. The barn belonged to a farmer called Abinadab. Abinadab's two sons got ready to take the Ark into the city. A new cart was made. Oxen were put into the shafts.

King David arrived with all the priests. They were going to lead the procession. Very carefully new poles were pushed through the golden rings on the sides of the sacred box. It was lifted from the ground and placed gently on top of the cart. The priests lined up and started to march. Right at the front was King David. The oxen leaned forward and the heavy cart started to move. The two sons walked alongside the cart, Ahio leading the oxen, Uzzah prodding them with his stick. As they walked along, the crowd at the front started to sing and dance.

Suddenly the cart lurched to one side. One wheel had sunk into a soft patch of ground. As the cart tipped, the Ark started to slide off. Without thinking Uzzah, who was nearest, put out his hands. They touched the Ark and he let out a great cry of pain.

The singing stopped. The procession came to a halt. Men rushed back to help. It was too late. Uzzah gave a final scream and fell to the ground. He was dead.

What had happened?

'It is the Ark,' said the priests. 'He has touched the sacred object. That is why he is dead.'

David was not so sure. Was God really like that? he asked himself. Or had Uzzah tried to hold back the Ark when it was too heavy for him? But the people believed the priests. They were frightened of this box. One thing was certain. The Ark would not be taken to Jerusalem today.

Nearby was a farm. All together the men pushed the ox-cart out of the soft earth, being careful not to touch its precious load. The cart was pushed into a barn. David went back to Jerusalem. His day was spoilt.

For three months the Ark stayed in the barn. Then David decided to try again. Very carefully the oxen were put back in the shafts. This time lots of men walked alongside the cart to steady it. They made their way towards the gates of Jerusalem. Once again the crowd began to sing and to dance.

Now everything went as David hoped. The day the Ark came to Jerusalem was a day never to be forgotten. Thousands of people lined the streets.

As the procession came through the gates, King David

himself could be seen dancing wildly in front of the Ark. All around him other people were dancing and singing too. People blew trumpets, crashed cymbals – anything to make a noise.

The Ark was taken to a special tent which had been put up. When it was safely inside, the people held a great feast. Everybody joined in. David was so happy he never gave a thought to being a king. He was still dancing around handing out food and sweets.

Very late that night David got back to his palace. Michal, one of Saul's daughters, was waiting for him. She looked very angry. David smiled at her.

She did not smile back. 'Disgusting,' she snorted, looking down her nose at him. 'Fancy you, a king, prancing around in the street like a common fool. It's not decent.'

The smile left David's face. He was suddenly both angry with Michal and sorry for her. 'Today,' he said, 'was the day that all our ancestors from the time of Moses have wanted to see. It is the end of all our wandering in the desert. The Ark has come to Jerusalem. Why shouldn't we dance and be merry? Worshipping God doesn't mean we have to be miserable.'

Michal sniffed and walked away. David laughed. Poor Michal. She must be the only person in all Jerusalem who couldn't enjoy herself.

NOTES

ABOUT THE STORY

To bring Israel's most sacred object into the new capital was what would make Jerusalem the recognized centre. Not only the king but God himself would live there.

Here as elsewhere, David shows himself to be sensitive to the idea that Israel's king is different – subordinate to God and to divine law. Today we often speak of the rule of law as if it were a modern invention of Western democracies. It has deep roots in the traditions of the ancient world.

The first attempt to move the Ark proves abortive. We switch immediately from a sophisticated concept like the rule of law to taboo bordering on superstition. The biblical account strongly suggests that Uzzah died as a direct result of touching the sacred Ark. It is easy to dismiss such notions out of hand but in many parts of the world today there would still be, at the least, a reverent agnosticism towards such an interpretation.

The second attempt is successful but David's show of ecstasy proves unpopular with Michal. What comes through again is his natural humanity. He lets go and makes a fool of himself, apparently not only dancing but dancing naked in the street.

Excesses apart, the incident raises the question of festival and puritanism in religion. Puritanism, represented here by Michal, holds that there must be strict and sober self-control at all times, especially among leaders. For David, genuine celebration is spontaneous, breaking through normal inhibitions and conventions. Is morality about rules and decorum or about relationships and the celebration of life?

IDEAS FOR EXPLORING FURTHER

Holy Objects   What experiences do children have of items 'not to be touched' among their parents' possessions at home? What makes a thing precious? Is it how much it cost or its associations? Talk with older pupils about the reverence of Sikhs, Muslims and Jews for their sacred writings and investigate other religious artefacts. Discuss the reserved sacrament in a Roman or Anglo-Catholic church.

Worship   Use video/pictures, invite visitors or make visits to help children compare two different ways of worshipping (e.g. the silence of Quakers; the elaborate and solemn rituals of the Greek Orthodox and Roman Catholic Church; the raising of hands and dancing of members of some evangelical groups; the colourful symbolism of Hindus; the precise rituals of Muslims and Jews). Use sacred music to illustrate contrasts. Draw out specialist vocabulary.

Story-telling through Dance   Make up a dance sequence to illustrate the story. For example:

(i) entering the dusty barn, pushing clutter aside (slow, fluid, dream-like movements, alternating high and low in search of the Ark, reverence when it is found);

(ii) making a new cart, bringing the oxen (staccato actions and beats to denote lifting, sawing, hammering, feet of oxen);

(iii) accompanying the Ark with joy as it sets out on its first journey (a sequence of high/low/middle-level actions performed in small groups, to represent the unity of the people, accompanied by vibrant and quite impressive music);

(iv) panic when the cart lurches and Uzzah is killed (unmelodic sounds, spiky, jerky body shapes leading to a 'freeze' in a scrunched-up position);

(v) recovery and deciding to try again (a silence, followed by gentle expansive music and slow 'unwinding' actions);

(vi) the final entry of the Ark into Jerusalem (majestic music, two sequences of actions to indicate unity and security – repeat the earlier one and add a new one).

In discussion, draw out people's feelings and reactions to the different parts of the story.

26

You Are the Man

2 Samuel 11: 1 – 12: 13

It was springtime. David sat out on the roof of his house in the middle of Jerusalem. It was quiet. Most of the young men had gone away with the army to fight the Ammonites. They were trying to capture the city of Rabbah. David's time of leading the army was over. As king he had to stay behind in the capital but he was bored.

He stood up and walked around the rooftop, idly looking down on the streets below and on other houses not as tall as his. It was then that he saw her. Down in the courtyard of one of the houses a woman was washing herself. Surrounded by the four walls she thought she was private and alone. It had not occurred to her to look upwards. She stretched out her limbs in the sunshine as she washed and dried herself. David's attention was held. Then she finished and went indoors.

David called one of his servants. He pointed to the house and asked, 'Who lives there?' It was the house of Uriah, one of David's officers who was away with the army. The woman was his wife Bathsheba. David had many wives, as was the custom for rich and powerful men, but he knew he wanted Bathsheba as well. He sent for her to come and visit him. She was brought to the palace. He was the king. She could hardly refuse.

A little while later she sent a message to David. It said, 'I am going to have a baby. You are the father.' Even though David was the king he was frightened. What could he do? If people discovered that Bathsheba had been going with another man while her husband was away at the war then she would probably be stoned to death, even though it was David's fault, not hers. The law was very unfair to women.

David sent a message to Joab, the commander of his army. 'Send home Uriah on leave,' it said. 'I want to know how our campaign is going and he is the best officer to tell me.'

Uriah returned and gave David a full account. 'Splendid,' said David. 'Now go home to your wife. Take a few days' more leave. You have deserved it.'

But Uriah did not go home. David found out next morning that he had stayed in the guardhouse of his own palace. He could not understand it until Uriah explained. 'All my friends and comrades are living rough and dangerously near the battlefront,' he said. 'It would be wrong for me to be enjoying good food, a comfortable bed and the company of my wife while they are all suffering.'

David tried in all sorts of ways to make him change his mind but it was no use. Uriah was a dedicated soldier.

Next morning Uriah was all ready to go back to the army. David gave him a sealed letter for General Joab. Uriah was such a faithful soldier that David knew he would not open it. It was Uriah's death warrant. It told the general to put Uriah in charge of a suicide squad with orders to go right up underneath the city walls to attack the Ammonites.

The general did as he was told. The men had little chance. They had no protection and were easy targets. One of them was even killed by a woman pushing a millstone over the wall on top of him. Uriah was among those killed.

When the news came back to David he sent again for Bathsheba. This time she moved into his house and became one of his wives. Now when the baby was born it would be seen as the child of a queen. David heaved a great sigh of relief.

A few days later Nathan asked to speak to David. Nathan was a rough-looking figure, but he was known to be a good man. He was a prophet who was believed to speak for God. David agreed to see him.

The two men sat alone. 'What is it you want?' asked David. Nathan paused, fixed his eyes on the king and told him a story. 'There were two men, one rich, one poor,' he began. 'The rich man had large flocks of sheep; the poor man had one little ewe lamb which he had had to save up to buy. One day the rich man had a visitor. He knew he had to entertain the visitor to dinner but he did not want to slaughter one of his own sheep. So he sent out one of his workers to steal the poor man's lamb, kill it and turn it into stew for the meal. The poor man was terribly upset and so were his children. Their one lamb was more like a family pet than anything else.'

David listened to the story with growing anger. Finally he leaped from his chair and shouted, 'Who is this rich man? He will pay for this. He deserves to die for that sort of thing.'

There was a long silence. Then Nathan spoke just four words. 'You are the man,' he said. There was an even longer silence. Nathan wondered if now it was he who would have to die.

David finally spoke. 'You are right,' he said, 'It is a terrible thing that I have done.'

——————————————— **NOTES** ———————————————

ABOUT THE STORY

The core of this story lies in the final confrontation between Nathan and David in which David, although king, yields to the moral authority of the prophet and accepts the judgement made upon him. It is a classic case of the rule of divine law and the place of kingship in Israel. It is also a key story about the dignity and equality of women.

However, to understand properly the ending the full gravity of the narrative which leads up to it has to be spelt out. It is a story of adult emotions and adult temptation. For this reason previous generations have tended to omit this incident from children's anthologies. Times have changed but even now some may find it difficult. Just how much detail is entered into must depend on individual relationships between teacher and pupils.

The seduction of Bathsheba and the attempted cover-up leads to the deaths of innocent men. Ironically it is David's sense of guilt and his refusal to play the despot which, together with Uriah's virtuous and utterly loyal behaviour, exacerbates the whole situation. The alternative would have been to blame the woman. Had Bathsheba been deserted she would probably have been stoned to death for adultery. It is a story which has been repeated again and again in the history of human affairs with a variety of outcomes.

David's eventual punishment is that he will not achieve his highest aspiration: to build the Temple. That privilege goes to Solomon, his later son by Bathsheba after the death, in extreme infancy, of the child born as a result of this incident – a final touch of irony and itself seen as a punishment.

However, despite everything, David's repentance and his acceptance of the prophet's judgement serves, in Jewish eyes, to ensure his greatness. It is his reign, not Solomon's, which continues to be seen as the Golden Age of Israel. In the moral and religious sphere God's rule, rather than the king's, still held sway.

IDEAS FOR EXPLORING FURTHER

The Ten Commandments   Go back to Story 14 and look at the Ten Commandments to see how many David broke through his dealings with Uriah and Bathsheba.

Selfishness   Discuss events from Bathsheba's point of view. Did David ask her what she would like? Perhaps she loved Uriah and did not want to leave him, let alone have him killed. Maybe she did not want to move into a strange household and spend the majority of her life with a completely different set of people. Think of times when selfishness makes people unhappy (cf. *The Selfish Giant*, by Oscar Wilde).

Truth   It often comes out sooner or later. Collectively or in groups, make up a story in which people tell lies about an event or try to cover it up and then the truth comes out. Perhaps one of the characters is even brave enough to own up. Act out the story, or make a clay model to represent the moment when the truth is told. (■ *English*) Wrongdoing often brings its own rewards. (Cf. Story 28.)

27

A House for God – for Kings and Horses Too

1 Kings 6: 11–37; 7: 1–12; 9: 15–28

David had done many deeds that were to be remembered for ever. His reign over Israel was to become known as 'The Golden Age'. He had beaten the Philistines, captured Jerusalem, and brought the Ark of the Covenant at last into the holy city. It still needed a home which was better than a tent. David had not built a Temple where it could be kept.

As soon as he became king, Solomon, David's son, set to work. Plans were drawn. The Jerusalem Temple was to be like the desert Tabernacle but it would be made of stone. There would be three parts: the courtyard, the place of sacrifice and the Holy of Holies where the Ark would rest.

King Solomon walked around the site. 'This is a holy place,' he said. 'It is the place where Abraham brought Isaac many years ago. There must be no noise here while the Temple is being built. The workmen must work in silence.'

That made work very difficult. All the huge blocks of stone had to be shaped at the quarry where they were cut. Then they had to be dragged to the site and fitted together without any hammering.

There were no lorries or cranes; there was no dynamite for blasting rocks. Everything had to be done by hand. At the quarry men with hammers and chisels made cracks in the rock. Into the cracks they drove wooden wedges. Water was poured on to the wedges. Sometimes it took hours; often it took days; but sooner or later the wedges would swell out with the water and the rock would split. Then began the long task of shaping the stone to fit the pieces around it.

The stones were pulled to Jerusalem on sledges. Then they had to be lifted into position. To do this the men would sometimes have to build large ramps of earth and drag new stones to the top of the half-built wall.

The work took seven years. Men from every tribe took it in turns to do the work. They would work for a month and then go back to their farms for two months. There were no wages and sometimes their own crops were spoilt, but it was work for God and everybody joined in.

When it was all finished there was the greatest festival anybody had ever seen. The Ark was carried in a great procession and placed in the Holy of Holies. There it could stay for ever. In the streets there was singing and dancing.

But King Solomon did not dance in the street like his father David had done. He was much too proud. Besides, he had other ideas. He liked the Temple and was very pleased with the way it stood on the highest point in Jerusalem. Wouldn't it be nice, he thought, if I had lots of other buildings like it? Then other kings would come here and see how rich and powerful I was.

After the celebrations the men of Israel were looking forward to getting back to their own farms. Solomon had other ideas. He made them start all over again. This time it was for a palace for himself. The Temple was big; the palace was even bigger. It took twelve years to build.

Then there were the stables. Solomon loved horses. He had hundreds of them. The stables that were built were almost like another palace. Foreign princes came from everywhere to look at all Solomon's riches. Even the Queen of Sheba from the centre of Africa heard about him and came to look at all these splendid buildings.

Next Solomon had a whole fleet of ships built. He really was becoming a great king. But he did not notice that the people had begun to hate him. The labour gangs had become more and more cruel. Men felt they were slaves again. Even

113

worse, there were favourites among them. The tribes from the north were being made to work far harder than the tribes from the south.

The Israelites had become one nation under David. Now the northerners were ready to rebel. They found a leader. His name was Jeroboam.

NOTES

ABOUT THE STORY

The significance of finally building and opening the Temple cannot be exaggerated. For centuries it was the focal point of what was to become known as Judaism and even today the Western Wall retains a special place in the minds of Jews throughout the world. The sacrifice involved in building it must have been enormous and is to be compared with the effort which went into medieval cathedrals.

Solomon's place in history was ensured by this one act but otherwise his reign was something of a disaster. His accession to the throne as David's son marked the end of a dynasty as Israel moved closer to the habits of surrounding nations. As the previous story shows, the struggle for supremacy in moral leadership was not over but there appears no longer to have been a religious leader of the stature of Samuel to keep kingship in its place.

Solomon became an Eastern potentate with a somewhat spurious reputation for wisdom, apparently based on the one story in 1 Kings 3: 16–28 (a story to be found in Indian as well as in Jewish mythology), but with a quite genuine one for building up enormous wealth, power and prestige. The visit of the Queen of Sheba (Ethiopia) recorded in 1 Kings 10 illustrates this and the final verdict on his reign is given in 1 Kings 11: 9–13. Note that the Jews of Ethiopia who were evacuated to modern Israel in the 1980s have their origins in this relationship.

Solomon appears to have possessed little of the devotional simplicity of David. He had never had to struggle but, as so often happens in history, having inherited power he was able to retain it during his own lifetime. The simmering resentment, particularly of the northern tribes, begins to surface in this story but it was only after his death that it exploded.

IDEAS FOR EXPLORING FURTHER

Religious Buildings   What do people try to express in the design of religious buildings, the materials used and the decoration? All kinds of questions could be asked. For example, does the shape of a spire/minaret try to direct our attention towards God? Why is a Christian church often cross-shaped? What is the significance of an altar in

114

such a church and why is it often placed at the east end of the building? When considering a mosque, children could consider why and how the direction of Makkah is shown there. Could the arches be thought of as doorways between earthly and heavenly spheres? Many religious buldings are constructed in stone. Perhaps the children could suggest a reason for this. Could it be that stone symbolizes the strength of God or the loyalty of God's people? Some religious buildings are decorated 'fit for a king'. Why are precious gems/metals and rich colours often used? What do religious symbols represent (e.g. power, sacrifice, love, holiness)? Why are sacred writings kept in a special place in a synagogue or gurdwara? Pupils could visit two places of worship and compare them. They could also design and make a model of a religious building. (▮NC▮ *Technology; History:* SSU on houses and places of worship) Extension work might include exploring types and uses of materials (▮NC▮ *Science*) and investigating the characteristics of different types of stone (▮NC▮ *Geography:* AT 3 – physical geography).

Shapes   How does a circle represent the 'wheel of life' for Buddhists? Discuss meanings of the cross shape, the star of David, the Hindu 'Om' and reversed swastika signs. Talk about why Muslims prefer geometric patterns and refuse to draw Muhammad. (▮NC▮ *Mathematics:* number, measures, shape and space, handling data: e.g. explore two- and three-dimensional shapes observed in religious buildings or pictures; consider symmetry, tessellation, fractions and measurements; help older pupils to make geometric patterns and to work on angles and fractions.)

28

A Stupid Young Man

1 Kings 12: 1–16

As long as Solomon was alive the tribes of the north could do nothing. They wanted to rebel but Solomon was too strong. Their leader, Jeroboam, had to run away to Egypt.

At last King Solomon died. His son Rehoboam was to take his place. Rehoboam was made king by his own tribes in the south. Then he went to the town of Shechem in the north to be crowned again. It was there that Rehoboam met Jeroboam who had now returned from Egypt.

Jeroboam spoke quite openly. 'Your father Solomon was a real slave-driver,' he said. 'If you promise to treat us better and stop all this slavery we shall be happy for you to be our king as well.'

Rehoboam was thoughtful. 'Give me three days to think about it,' he said at last. The people agreed and he went away.

Rehoboam called together his father's advisers. They were old and wise. 'What shall I do?' he asked them.

'A real king is the servant of the people,' they replied. 'He has to lead the people, but he must always be one of them and not make himself high and mighty. If you treat them kindly the northerners will be loyal.'

Rehoboam listened politely but he did not like it. He was a young hothead. He sent the old advisers away and went to see his friends who were young like him. He asked them what they thought.

'Show them who is the boss,' they said without thinking.

116

'You're the king. Don't give in. Be tough and put them in their place.'

Rehoboam liked that advice. It made him feel important. Those silly old fools were past it. It was time they were all sacked.

Three days later the assembly met again at Shechem. Rehoboam sat up on the platform. He was surrounded by his friends.

The northern leaders stepped forward. 'Tell us,' they said, 'what is your answer to our question? Will you treat us better than your father did, or not?'

Rehoboam sat there. He looked them up and down. 'Treat you better!' he sneered. 'Who do you think you are to talk to me like that? I'm not going to make your life any easier at all. In fact I'm going to make it a lot harder. You've seen nothing yet. Listen.'

He started to shout. He stood and held up the little finger of his right hand. 'See that,' he shouted. 'My little finger is going to be thicker than my father's thighs. He hit you with whips. I'm going to whip you with scorpions.'

His friends laughed. It was not a nice laugh. Rehoboam joined in. He sat down again. He obviously felt very pleased with himself.

Jeroboam and the other northern leaders turned away. It was no good arguing. 'Come on,' they said. 'We can have nothing more to do with David's kingdom. It's not for us any more.'

They turned and left.

Rehoboam sent for Adoram. He had been in charge of the old labour gangs. He was a hard, cruel man, the biggest slave-driver of them all.

'Take some soldiers,' ordered Rehoboam, 'and put down their little rebellion. Arrest their leaders and teach them a lesson.'

Rehoboam went off with his friends. 'Good old Rehoboam,' they were saying. 'That will show them. We'll rule the country now. We're not going to be pushed around by a bunch of peasants.'

They were still laughing when a soldier staggered in. His head was bleeding.

'What is it?' asked Rehoboam. 'What's the matter? Where's Adoram?'

'He's dead,' gasped the soldier.

'Dead!' echoed Rehoboam.

'Yes,' said the soldier. 'The crowd wouldn't obey us. When we tried to arrest the leaders they started to stone us. We hadn't a chance. I only just managed to escape. They are angry and coming this way.'

Rehoboam's friends were no longer laughing. They looked scared. 'Quick. Let's get out of here,' they shouted.

And off they ran.

Rehoboam jumped into his chariot. The driver lashed the horses. They broke into a gallop. As Jeroboam and his friends came over the hill all they could see of Rehoboam was a cloud of dust in the distance on the road south.

The northerners looked for their own king. They chose Jeroboam. Now there were two countries where before there had been one. The north was called Israel. The south was called Judah. Nobody was happy about it. The northerners were as sad as anybody. They made up a song, a song of lament. It went like this.

> We don't belong to David,
> We have nothing to do with Jesse's son.
> Back to your own homes you men of the north,
> Let David's people go their own way.

ABOUT THE STORY

Historically speaking this story is of great importance. The Division of the Kingdom took place in 937 B.C.E. The ten northern tribes retained the name of Israel but separated themselves off from Jerusalem and the Davidic dynasty. Jeroboam, who had come to prominence when he represented their pleas to Solomon and had been forced to take refuge in Egypt, was anointed as their king. Since the northerners felt cut off from Jerusalem, a new centre had to be found. Eventually it was to be Samaria.

The Southern Kingdom now consisted of only two tribes, Benjamin and Judah (see p. 49 and map on p.ii). The latter name was taken for the whole and so, in time, the name of Jew, or citizen of Judah, began to emerge.

It is the northern tribes who, at this point, have remained closest to the earlier beliefs of Israel. Rehoboam's stance is exactly the one which Samuel had feared and tried to warn against. Moral and religious leadership was no longer to be found among the ruling class, which had become despotic.

IDEAS FOR EXPLORING FURTHER

Choices   (Cf. Stories 10, 21.) What would have happened if Rehoboam had taken the elders' advice? Would the whole course of history have been different? Make a list of situations where people might have to make choices. For each one, ask groups of children to put their ideas on cards or draw pictures and make a mobile, indicating on it the situation to be faced, the possible choices and their probable results. For example:

Situation   I have broken a window.

Choice 1   I could keep quiet.
Result   Someone else may be blamed. I might feel bad about that.

Choice 2   I could blame someone else.
Result   They will be unjustly punished and both God and I will know the truth. Also, the truth may be found out and then I may be punished for breaking the window *and* lying. Parents may be disappointed in me.

Choice 3   I could own up.
Result   I may be punished, but at least people will respect me for owning up.

Extravagance   Look at magazine and newspaper pictures of people with different lifestyles. Rank the pictures first to indicate priority 'needs' as opposed to 'wants', then to show those whose lifestyle is the most luxurious/extravagant. Discuss reasons for choices. Which are the crucial needs? How much is enough? (██ *Geography*: AT 2 – effects of wealth on daily life) If you had unlimited time, money, labour, skill, what would you build and why?

29

Naboth's Vineyard

1 Kings 21

When Ahab became king of Israel he married Jezebel. Jezebel was a princess from Phoenicia and she was well known for her bad temper.

Today she stormed into Ahab's room. 'What's the matter with you?' she demanded.

'Nothing,' muttered Ahab. He was sulking.

'Nothing!' screamed Jezebel. 'What do you mean, nothing? You haven't eaten a thing all day.'

There was a silence. Then Ahab said, 'It's Naboth.'

'Who is Naboth?' Jezebel asked.

'He's the owner of that vineyard next to my summer palace, the vineyard I wanted to buy to make my garden bigger.'

'Oh, him,' said Jezebel. 'Is that all? And why should a king be all sulky about a little farmer?'

'He won't sell me the vineyard, that's why,' protested Ahab. 'He says it's always belonged to his family and he doesn't want to move.'

Jezebel's eyes blazed. 'What do you mean, he won't sell it? You're king aren't you? Just take it. My father would, but then he's strong, not a little weakling like you.'

Ahab sighed. 'You don't understand,' he said. 'In Israel the king can't just do what he likes. God is the real king and I have to obey the law just like anyone else.'

'Well, I'm not an Israelite,' snorted Jezebel, 'even if I married one. I'll get your vineyard for you.'

Ahab started to argue but she stormed out and slammed the door. Oh, well, he thought, it's her, not me. I can't stop her. He lay down on the bed again.

Jezebel sat at her desk. She thought for a moment. Then she reached for her pen and paper and wrote a short letter. She addressed it to the elders and nobles of the city. A messenger was called and the letter was sent on its way.

Naboth was working in his vineyard when the soldiers arrived. He was arrested and dragged to the city square where all the elders were waiting. A court had been set up. Naboth did not know what was happening until the chief elder spoke.

'Naboth,' he said, 'it is a serious crime in this country to curse God as well as the king. In fact it carries the death penalty. Now what have you got to say?'

Naboth looked all around him. Suddenly he was very frightened.

'I've no idea what you are talking about, sir,' he said. 'I've never cursed God or the king – or anybody else for that matter,' he added.

'But we have witnesses,' said the chief elder. He made a signal with his hand.

Two scruffy beggars were pushed to the front of the crowd. 'That's him,' cried one, pointing to Naboth. 'Yes, that's him, no doubt about it. We were going past the vineyard when we heard this dreadful noise. We looked over and there he was cursing God and swearing about the king. Dreadful things he was saying. He said –'

'That's enough,' interrupted the elder. 'Naboth,' he said, 'we find you guilty.' He turned to the crowd. 'Take him away and stone him to death,' he said.

Naboth was pulled away and chased out of the square. He was knocked over and the crowd threw stones at him until he was dead. The two beggars shuffled away, counting the money they had been given to tell lies.

Back at the palace Jezebel went to see Ahab again. 'All right,' she said, 'you can go and look at your vineyard. Naboth's no longer around.'

'What's happened ... ?' Ahab began.

But Jezebel cut him short. 'Don't ask questions' was all she said.

Ahab shrugged his shoulders. 'Well, it wasn't my fault,' he said to himself, but he wasn't sure.

It was evening when Ahab got to the vineyard. The sun was going down and it was cool. The vineyard was beautiful. He picked some grapes. Delicious!

Suddenly he felt someone behind him. He turned round. There in the shadows stood a large figure. He was tall with big shoulders. He had a long beard and carried a staff. Ahab didn't have to ask who it was. He knew. It was the prophet Elijah. Everyone accepted him as God's spokesman.

Ahab didn't know what to say. In the end he muttered, 'You've found me, then?'

'I've found you, all right,' thundered Elijah. 'And I have this to say to you from God himself. You're not fit to be king of his people. The day is not far off when you will die as violently as Naboth did today. You are criminals, both you and Jezebel.'

Elijah turned and strode away. Ahab shuddered. Elijah had frightened him.

He went back to the palace still trembling. There he told Jezebel what had happened. She was furious, but she was a bit frightened too. There was only one way out. She must kill Elijah as well.

ABOUT THE STORY

The next few stories (29–32) are about the Northern Kingdom of Israel. The town of Samaria had been made into the capital by King Omri (887–875 B.C.E.) and the long rivalry between Jews in Jerusalem and those living in Samaria, who were to become Samaritans, had begun.

Ahab was the immediate successor to Omri. His wife was the notorious Jezebel, a princess of Phoenicia, part of modern Lebanon. Her name has become synonymous with vindictiveness. A popular song of the 1950s included the lines: 'If ever a devil was born without a pair of horns, it was you, Jezebel, it was you.'

'Naboth's Vineyard' is an important story. First, it introduces Elijah, who in Jewish esteem ranks with Moses. Between them they represent prophecy and law. The final scene of this story shows Elijah, like Nathan before him, thundering against the king himself. In the Bible a prophet is a *forth*teller, not a *fore*teller. His authority is a moral authority; he has no status or position other than that of being recognized as a spokesman for God. Many prophets were persecuted and killed but those who inflicted suffering on the prophets were felt to be damned.

Secondly, this story returns to two, by now, familiar themes, the threat of belief in other gods and the question of the role of the king. Elijah's message to Ahab in modern parlance is simply: 'God rules – O.K.?'

Thirdly, we gain a valuable insight into the sacred nature of land. Ahab recognizes that Naboth is perfectly within his rights. The land is held in trust from God. To sell land would be to sell one's children's birthright. Jezebel's solution could belong to almost any age or place. It is evil and someone must confront and expose it even at the cost of personal suffering. Elijah accepts the role.

IDEAS FOR EXPLORING FURTHER

God's Law   If this had been obeyed, what would have been the outcome? Retell/ rewrite the story from this perspective. Discuss/write the contents of Jezebel's letter, indicating her feelings while writing it. (NC *English*: ATs 1, 3)

Lying   Discuss the beggars' motives. Did they have reasons for lying? Consider real crimes and motives. Does poverty force people into crime? (NC *Geography*: AT 2 – effects of wealth)

30

The Contest on Mount Carmel

1 Kings 18: 7 – 19: 3

Elijah was on the run. He had hidden in the mountains. Queen Jezebel had soldiers looking everywhere for him. There were other prophets, men who were not afraid to speak out. Some of those Jezebel had had killed.

From his hiding-place Elijah saw someone coming along the mountain track. He recognized him. It was Obadiah, another prophet. Elijah ran down to meet him.

They greeted one another and then Elijah said, 'Will you go to King Ahab and ask him to come out and meet me here?'

'King Ahab!' gasped Obadiah. 'But haven't you heard how his wife Jezebel is trying to kill all the prophets? She will have me murdered.'

'I don't think so,' replied Elijah. 'I'm the one she really wants, and they won't harm you if the king thinks you can lead him to me.'

In the end Obadiah agreed. Some time later he returned with the king. Ahab and Elijah stood facing one another as they had done in Naboth's vineyard.

'At last I have found you then, you trouble-maker,' said Ahab.

'It's you who are the trouble-maker,' replied Elijah. 'You and that heathen wife of yours. I hear she's bringing a whole lot of priests from her own country now. She's going to try to change our religion, is she?'

Ahab could not answer. He knew it was true but he was too weak to do anything about it.

'The time has come to put things to the test,' said Elijah. 'You can arrange a contest. Call all the people to Mount Carmel. Order Jezebel's priests to be there. Then we shall see which God is real.'

Ahab agreed. He was as frightened of Elijah as he was of Jezebel. As long as King Ahab was there Elijah was safe. Ahab would never harm a prophet, and Jezebel had no power when there were lots of people about.

The day came. Crowds of people gathered on the hillside. At the bottom stood Elijah. Facing him were all Jezebel's priests – about four hundred of them.

Elijah turned to the crowd. They went silent. 'You people of Israel,' he shouted. 'You are supposed to be the people of God but you keep forgetting all about him. You can't keep jumping about from one god to another. You've got to decide.'

He turned to face Jezebel's priests. 'We will build two altars,' he said. 'One to your god and one to mine, in order to make burnt offerings. But we shan't light the fires. The gods can do that.'

The priests of Baal (that's what their gods were called) collected stones and built an altar. Then they placed large slabs of meat on top. When they had done that they started to chant and dance. Elijah sat and watched them. The chanting went on and on. Nothing happened.

Elijah yawned. Then he called out, 'Sing louder. Perhaps Baal can't hear you.'

The priests of Baal began to get all worked up. They sang louder and danced faster.

'Come on,' called Elijah, 'he can't have gone far.'

The crowd started to laugh.

Elijah got more and more insulting. 'Louder,' he called, 'perhaps he's gone to the lavatory or maybe he's dozed off somewhere.'

The crowd roared with laughter. By now Jezebel's priests

125

were in a real frenzy. Some of them were so worked up they began to cut themselves. Still nothing happened.

Elijah stood up. 'Stop,' he called. 'It's my turn now.'

The screaming and chanting stopped. The priests sank to the ground exhausted. The crowd went quiet.

Elijah began to build his altar. 'See,' he called out, 'I take twelve stones for the twelve tribes of Israel.' He placed the meat on top. Then he fetched water, twelve jars of it and poured it all over. He raised his arms. Everything went very still. His voice carried over the hillside.

'O Lord God of Abraham, of Isaac and of Israel, let it be known today that you really are God in this land and that I am your servant.'

For a second nothing happened. Then from nowhere came a blinding flash and a roar of thunder. The altar was covered in flames.

The crowd on the hillside flattened themselves on the ground. People shook with fright.

Suddenly it was all over. The crowd went wild. They surged down the hillside. The priests of Baal saw them coming and tried to run for their lives. They were too late. Every one of them was caught.

Elijah thought he knew what to do next. He had all Jezebel's priests taken down to the Kishon brook at the bottom of the hill and killed.

It didn't help at all. When Jezebel heard what had happened she was in a terrible rage. She sent Elijah a message. It said: 'I swear by my gods that by this time tomorrow you will be as dead as my priests.'

With the excitement over, the crowd melted away. Elijah found he was all on his own again. His supporters were only brave when there was no danger. Jezebel was more determined than ever to get him. Sadly, he turned to the south and hurried away again. He was still on the run.

NOTES

ABOUT THE STORY

This is the first real miracle story we have encountered. There is no point in pretending that we can ever know exactly what happened or that we can simply explain it away. An early Agreed Syllabus (Cambridge 1949) described a miracle as 'any event which brings about an overwhelming sense of the presence of God'. Whatever its possible shortcomings, this definition draws us back to the central point that what happens inwardly is of greater religious significance than what can be shown to have occurred outwardly.

Jezebel had reintroduced the worship of the Baalim. No defence of Israel's faith was forthcoming from the king. Religious leadership had re-emerged separately in the form of the prophets but they were being persecuted and were in hiding. Chief amongst them was Elijah, who decides here that the time has come for a showdown.

Mount Carmel is a wooded promontory breaking up the smooth curve of the Palestinian coastline. Today it stands above the modern port of Haifa. At this time it marked the boundary between Israel and Phoenicia.

Two aspects of this story present difficulties. One is the actual means of ignition of the altar. We can only tell the story as it stands. We cannot know exactly *what* happened. However, something highly significant occurred which led to a revolt against Jezebel's priests and her imported religion.

The second difficulty is moral. Elijah still believes that destroying evil means the destruction of those in whom it resides. The priests of Baal are massacred like a herd of cattle with anthrax. It solves nothing. There is a negative moral lesson here: hatred breeds hatred. The incident merely hardens Jezebel's resolve for revenge. The showdown may have demonstrated the superior power of Israel's God. It has done nothing to demonstrate his moral superiority and the vicious circle remains unbroken.

IDEAS FOR EXPLORING FURTHER

Miracles   Discuss statements like 'She made a miraculous recovery', 'They made a miraculous escape', 'It's a miracle he wasn't hurt', 'Only a miracle can save them now', 'This medicine works miracles'. At times believers feel a strong sense of the hand of God. Are there modern miracles? Can pupils recall 'near misses' when they might have been hurt or stories about people making unexpected recoveries, people 'winning through' despite all odds (e.g. people buried by earthquake rubble for days), survivors of shipwrecks, train disasters, etc.? (See newspapers.) Talk about believers having faith in prayer to achieve miracles, particularly at places of pilgrimage (e.g. Lourdes, Walsingham, Benares, Amritsar, etc.). Here you can see stones bearing thanks for prayers/miracles granted. Discuss coincidences which some people feel are God's work (e.g. someone one day being asked to pay a gas bill they can't afford and the next receiving a gift or a rebate from another company).

Violence   Was revenge Elijah's only option? Could he have tried to win Ahab over with talk, or form a team of faithful people to convince others of the evil of Jezebel so that her priests and demands would go unheeded? Could he have prayed for wisdom before acting, or trusted God to deal with Jezebel? Talk about choices in daily life. Is it true that violence breeds violence? Talk about playground and sibling quarrels. Older children can consider Northern Ireland and South Africa. Does violence create more problems than it solves? Consider armed conflict currently in the news. (██ *History:* CSU 2 – Catholics/ Protestants, civil war; CSU 3 – the Empire; CSU 4 – Second World War).

31

A Voice of Gentle Stillness

1 Kings 19: 4–18

It was a long journey. For forty days Elijah had walked. He felt sad and very lonely as he travelled through the desert. Everything he had done had been a waste of time. Nobody believed in God any more. They were all frightened of Queen Jezebel. He must be the only loyal Israelite left and all he wanted to do was to die.

Elijah stood and looked up at the mountain. If he were going to find God anywhere surely it must be here. This was the holy place. It was here that Moses had first seen the glowing fire in the bush; it was here that he had led the people when he brought them out of Egypt; it was here that he had received the ten rules from God. This was Mount Sinai which every Israelite had heard about but none had visited since the time of Moses.

Elijah began to climb. Up and up he went. He looked down. Today there was nothing but desert stretching out as far as he could see. Once there were tents down there with thousands of people. Moses had received the commandments at this spot and looked down on the Israelites below. Now it was empty. It was as if all the Israelites had gone away from God just as they had gone away from this mountain.

Night came. The mountain suddenly felt hard and cruel, but in a strange way Elijah felt safe. If he were going to die, why not here where God had shown himself? He crept into a cave to sleep.

Suddenly he was wide awake. As if from nowhere God came to him. 'What are you doing here, Elijah?' he seemed to ask.

'O God,' replied Elijah, 'I've done everything I can. My people have forgotten all about you. I've worked and worked. With the other prophets I've risked my life and all for nothing. I think I'm the only one left alive who still tries to be loyal to you.'

'Go outside,' said the voice. 'I have a lesson to teach you.'

Elijah moved out of the cave. Everything was dark and black. Suddenly a wind sprang up. It got stronger and stronger. Soon it became so strong that it pushed Elijah back against the wall of the cave. He could hardly breathe. Small stones began to roll down the mountainside. They knocked against bigger stones and soon large stones followed them, tumbling and crashing to the bottom. It was as if some great powerful force were pushing the very mountain over. But Elijah felt nothing, just numb and miserable.

The wind died down. But suddenly the ground beneath Elijah's feet began to shake. There was a deep rumbling sound which came up from deep inside the mountain. The ground trembled and shook again. More stones began to fall. It was an earthquake. It seemed as if some mighty force which had been trapped inside when the earth was made was trying to break out. Again and again the mountain shook.

Still Elijah stood there. He had known winds and earthquakes before. Once upon a time he had felt them as the mighty force of God. Now he felt nothing at all. It was the same when the thunder crashed and the lightning sparked all around him. It meant nothing. He just felt more and more miserable. Perhaps he just couldn't feel God any more. Perhaps all his life had been for nothing. Perhaps God wasn't really there at all.

He was still thinking these thoughts when suddenly everything went quiet. The wind had gone, the shaking had stopped, there was no more thunder and lightning. Not a sound could be heard. It was so quiet that Elijah could hear his own heart beating. He forgot the world outside. He went inside himself.

That was it. Suddenly he knew. The silence was more frightening than the storm. He could forget earthquakes when they were over. He could shelter from storms and hide from wind and rain. But he couldn't run away from himself. That was where God was all the time, deep down inside himself.

Elijah felt tired but happy. I came here, he thought, to find God.

'But you're not alone,' said the voice from within. 'I am always with you and there are others as well. There are thousands who have not gone to worship Baal. People don't always shout about what they believe. It is often the quiet ones who are faithful.'

Elijah left the mountain. He was old and he must die soon, but he knew now that the faith of Israel would go on. 'Find me in the silence,' God had said. It was a good lesson.

NOTES

ABOUT THE STORY

It is in this story that Elijah faces up to the fact that nothing has been won in the previous incident. The great flamboyant gesture has achieved nothing more than one day's headlines. He is back where he started. Jezebel still reigns supreme. The faith of Israel is being destroyed before his very eyes. He has failed to rouse the people into action against her and what she stands for. He feels deserted and has, once again, to flee for his life.

This time he literally goes back to where it all started. Israel's God confronted Moses at Sinai, first in the incident of the burning bush, secondly in the delivery of the Ten Commandments. Perhaps his presence will be readily felt on that holy mountain.

From Mount Carmel to Mount Sinai is a long journey on foot through very inhospitable terrain. Once there Elijah follows the footsteps of Moses up onto the mountain itself. He is surely trying to recapture the initial experience and certainty of faith.

The forces of nature unleash themselves. Anyone who has been in open or mountainous country during a storm will be able to add imaginatively to what is described here. Nevertheless, Elijah remains unmoved and dejected. It is the silence which takes him by surprise. The search for God is an inward search. Not only is this true for Elijah himself but for others too. What people feel and believe is not easily judged by outward appearances. There were thousands who had not 'bowed the knee to Baal' even if they had kept their heads down and done nothing about it.

IDEAS FOR EXPLORING FURTHER

Retreats In his retreat, what were Elijah's concerns? Water, heat, animals, Naboth's death, Ahab's weakness, stopping Jezebel, guilt, loneliness, uncertainty? Make a sequence of paintings to show Elijah's journey and concerns. Can colours and shapes represent emotions? Find out about earthquakes (NC *Geography*: AT 3) to understand what Elijah would have experienced. Invite pupils to suggest places where people might usefully go for a quiet think. Do these places have anything in common? Discuss retreats for lay people and members of religious communities. In Thailand most boys spend some time, if only a few weeks, as a Buddhist monk.

Silence Spend a few minutes in quietness and discuss sounds heard, thoughts, feelings. Does it help to lie down, or have one's eyes closed? Talk about Hindus, Buddhists, Quakers and those in monastic orders who spend much time in meditation.

32

The Story of Amos

The Book of Amos

Amos was a shepherd. He looked after his sheep in the hills near the little village of Tekoa where he also had some fields of his own. He was not rich but he was content and happy with the life he led in the country.

From time to time he went into the towns and bigger cities to sell his wool and other produce. At first he used to enjoy these visits, but slowly he began to notice things which made him very unhappy.

It was this new idea called money which seemed to make things worse. Some people had always been richer than others, but now the gap was getting wider. Once he had bartered his goods. He just exchanged them for other things he wanted. Now he sold them for these pieces of metal. That was good. It made trading much easier. But not everybody understood it properly.

Some people had borrowed money. Then they found they couldn't pay it back. In the end they had had to sell their fields. Then they couldn't grow anything else to sell. So they borrowed more money. When they couldn't pay that back they had to do terrible things. Some had sold their children for slaves. Others had become slaves themselves to the money-lenders. Money should have made life easier. Because people were greedy it made it much worse.

Every time Amos went into the city things seemed worse. The rich looked richer; the poor looked poorer. There were

133

more and more beggars in the streets, more and more people dying of starvation. And nobody seemed to care. Merchants were selling husks instead of wheat. They cheated with wrong weights on their scales and, worst of all, they thought they were superior.

When they went to the Temple to worship God, these rich men took lots of offerings. 'God will be pleased with us for giving him all this,' they said to themselves. They looked down their noses at the poor people who had nothing left to give.

Amos knew this was all wrong, but what could he do about it? Things were different in the country. There people still lived as if they were all related to one another. Surely that was the way God wanted it to be.

God had to have a spokesman. Slowly Amos came to realize that it would have to be him. He didn't want to become a prophet, but in the end he knew God was inside him telling him to speak out.

One day he stood up in the market square. A crowd gathered round. They loved a story-teller or a speaker. This old countryman looked wild and good for a laugh.

'God says he is going to punish Damascus,' Amos began.

The crowd clapped. They didn't like the people of Damascus.

'God says he is going to punish the people of Gaza for their evil ways,' Amos went on.

The crowd cheered again.

Amos went on through all the names of the surrounding countries. The Edomites, the Ammonites and the Moabites were all going to suffer.

The crowd loved it. More people came to see what all the noise was about.

Amos stopped. He looked around. The crowd went silent. He waited until he was sure everybody was listening. Then he roared out, 'And God has told me this, "I will punish Israel for all her sins".'

Nobody cheered this time. Just a low murmuring was

heard. Then a voice called out, 'Why, what have we done? The Temple is always full of our burnt offerings.'

'God says this,' replied Amos. '"I hate, I despise your feasts".'

At this some of the crowd began to get angry.

But Amos went straight on. 'God will punish us,' he said, 'because he is a God who wants justice. We sell good people for silver. Children are sold just for the price of a pair of shoes. People are cheated right, left and centre. God is more concerned with the way we live than with burnt offerings. What he wants is justice.'

The crowd had started to thin out. Many people didn't like this sort of talk.

Amos held up a lead weight on a piece of string. 'You know what this is, don't you?' he asked.

'It's a plumb-line, the sort builders use,' came the answer.

'It tells you when a wall is upright. It's always true,' said Amos. 'God is a plumb-line. Israel is like a leaning wall. The further up it goes, the more it leans away from the true. What will happen to a wall like that?'

'In the end it will fall down. It will collapse.'

'And that's what will happen to us,' said Amos.

Again and again Amos spoke like this in the market-place. He used other pictures too, pictures like a basket of summer fruit. 'See this fruit,' he would say. 'What time of year is it when we pick fruit?'

'At the end of the summer,' the crowd would reply.

'That's like Israel,' Amos would say. 'Our sunny days are over. The bad days of winter lie ahead unless we change our ways.'

Amos went back to his sheep and his small farm.

Sadly, the people of Israel took no notice of Amos and other prophets like him. In the end they were destroyed. Their enemies the Assyrians conquered them.

The Assyrians took away all the people and spread them all

135

over their empire. Ten of the twelve tribes of Israel simply disappeared and were never heard of again. Two remained: Judah and Benjamin. They made up the tiny land of Judah around the city of Jerusalem. In time they came to be known as Jews.

NOTES

ABOUT THE STORY

Of all the prophets none are more important than those of the eighth century B.C.E., Amos and Hosea in the north, Isaiah and Micah in the south. And yet their stories are rarely told. This is because the Bible gives us only their prophetic utterances, which read like sermons. The story-line has to be created from what we know of the socio-economic background of the time.

Somewhere around this time came the introduction of money with all the changes that that forces upon a tribal society. Age-old assumptions of community and corporateness were undermined. Land, always occupied in trust, became a personal possession. Class structures changed rapidly. Those who possessed money and land became rich. Others, deprived of land in an agricultural economy, quickly fell into hopeless poverty. In extreme cases this led to prostitution and slavery. On top of all this came religious hypocrisy. The rich offered greater gifts at the altars and the poor were made to feel morally as well as socially inferior.

To the eighth-century prophets this state of affairs represented a threat just as great as the Baalim and the Philistines in the past. These prophets preached a message of ethical monotheism. That is to say, God is one and his essential nature is moral. Ritual and sacramental offerings may have their place in religion but only for as long as they are based on right living. Without that they are meaningless. For Amos this meant preaching justice; for Hosea, loving-kindness.

Their message went unheeded. The Northern Kingdom of Israel fell apart socially then finally disappeared after Assyrian invasions from 737 B.C.E. onwards. Assyrian power was based on a policy of deportation of captive peoples. Thousands were forcibly moved and scattered. At this point the ten northern tribes simply vanish from the pages of history.

IDEAS FOR EXPLORING FURTHER

Money   Where does money come from? Discuss management of pocket-money/savings, and with older pupils the pros and cons of money-lending, interest, credit and debt. Who becomes richer/poorer? How important are money and goods today? Will these alone make you happy? Should we share our money (cf. Scrooge)? Look at what a charity spends money on. How do values and demand for goods affect prices? (NC *Economic and Industrial Understanding; Mathematics*: money)

Poverty   List reasons why people in Tekoa might have become poor: unemployment, crop failure, illness, accident, theft, prices going up but income remaining the same, more mouths to feed, other people not wanting the goods they had to sell, quarrels leading to people leaving home. How are poor people (homeless, beggars, tramps) viewed today? Link with the past. (NC *History*: CSU 2 – Elizabethan poor; CSU 3 – Victorian Britain) What happens to poor people living in countries where there is no social security? (NC *Geography*: AT 2)

Cheating   Ask children about different forms of cheating. Discuss how you can deceive others but you can't deceive God or yourself. You have to live with your own conscience. Which are the worst forms of cheating in the world today? (E.g. selling sub-standard goods, raising petrol prices before old stocks are used, stealing goods and selling them on, pretending drugs are not harmful, making false insurance and social-security claims, bank fraud, con men.) If enough people cheat, what will happen?

33

A Treasure-hunt in the Temple

2 Kings 22: 1–13; 23: 4–14 (Deuteronomy 28)

Josiah was only eight years old when he became king of the tiny land of Judah. The Israelites of the north had disappeared, taken away by the Assyrians.

Josiah took over from his grandfather, Manasseh, who was one of the worst kings ever known. He had forgotten all about the God of Abraham and Moses. Manasseh put up all sorts of idols. He even put up one outside Jerusalem to a god called Moloch. Moloch was supposed to like human sacrifices. Inside the idol a fire burned and at times human babies were fed into the flames.

Manasseh had no time for prophets. He was proud that the streets of Jerusalem ran with their blood.

Josiah was different. When he became king he looked around and decided that things had to change.

The Temple was in a terrible mess. It was starting to fall down. There were cracks in the walls and some of the pillars had collapsed. Inside there was dust and dirt everywhere. There wasn't much else inside. Most of the golden treasures had been taken away and melted down. Even the huge doors had been stripped of the gold and silver which had covered them.

Josiah sent for the High Priest. 'Get a wooden chest,' he said. 'Cut a hole in the top and put it outside the Temple door. Then let everybody know that we want money to repair and clean up the Temple.'

It worked. The people had hated Manasseh. Every night the box was full and in a very short time there was enough money to start the work.

Josiah sent for his secretary and gave his orders. 'Go down to the Temple,' he said. 'Tell Hilkiah, the High Priest, to give the money to the builders and carpenters so that they can start work.'

'You're not going to give them the money before they do the work, are you?' asked the secretary in amazement.

'Why not?' said Josiah. 'It's time we trusted people. It's their Temple as much as it is ours.'

Shaphan, the secretary, went down to the Temple. Hilkiah was there. He was reading a scroll. Shaphan started to give him the King's message. Hilkiah went on reading. He didn't seem interested in anything else.

'Did you hear what I said?' asked Shaphan.

The High Priest looked up. 'Oh yes, yes,' he said. 'Give the money to the workmen and tell them to get on with it.' He still went on reading.

Shaphan went off to talk to the workmen. The High Priest's manners were getting worse.

When Shaphan came back the High Priest was just finishing reading the scroll. He was very excited. 'You must read this,' he said, pushing the scroll into the secretary's hands. 'It has been found under a pile of rubbish in the Temple.'

Shaphan took the scroll. He went back to the palace to report to the King. As he was about to leave he gave the scroll to the King. 'Hilkiah gave me this,' he said. 'It's been found under some rubbish in the Temple. You'd think it was treasure the way Hilkiah was getting excited about it.'

'Read it to me,' replied Josiah.

Shaphan stood in front of the King and read aloud from the scroll. As he read, the King became more and more restless. The words of the scroll were a set of laws, like the Ten Commandments of Moses. They told of all the dreadful things which had happened to the ten tribes of the north. They warned that the same thing could happen to Judah.

When Shaphan finished reading there was a silence. Then Josiah said, 'It's not enough to rebuild the Temple. These words were written by some of the prophets my grandfather killed. We must do what they say. God doesn't just want a clean Temple. He wants us to treat other people properly.'

Josiah did all he could. He smashed all the idols to false gods. The huge idol to Moloch was broken down and turned into a rubbish-tip. Most of all, Josiah tried to rule with justice and mercy, to set an example. The people of Judah respected him. He was better than any other king they had known. Perhaps he would become a great king like David, they thought.

But it was not to be. Josiah was killed in battle while he was still a young man. Without him to lead, it began to look again as if Judah would make all the mistakes that the northern tribes had made.

ABOUT THE STORY

We now take up the story back in the Southern Kingdom. In 640 B.C.E. in Jerusalem the long reign of King Manasseh, the latest in a line of undesirable monarchs stretching back to Rehoboam, had at last come to an end. Suddenly there was hope again. His grandson, Josiah, began to show signs of a return to the principles of King David.

Things were in a poor state. The Temple was falling apart for lack of care. Religious leadership had ceased to be effective for fear of persecution. Under Manasseh, not only had prophets been killed but religion had sunk as low as it could go. Human sacrifice, supposedly abandoned back in the days of Abraham, had once again been practised. The king had led the way, making a burnt offering of one of his own sons (see 2 Kings 21: 6).

Josiah sets in motion a return to decency, symbolized by his trust in the ordinary people. A start is made on the restoration of the Temple. It is there that the great discovery is made. The prophets may have been silenced in the streets but not 'on paper'. What is discovered is a second (*deutero*) edition of the account of Jewish tradition and law (*nomos*). Deuteronomy is a rewrite of the whole Exodus story, accounting for, and giving meaning to, subsequent history. In trying, like Elijah, to recapture the spirit of the past, it reads as if written by Moses himself but there are good reasons for putting a much later date on it. The literary device fails altogether when the death of Moses is recorded.

Deuteronomy represents a highly developed legal and moral code, especially bearing in mind its time and context. All aspects of life are covered, including detailed instructions for the observance of major Jewish festivals (Deuteronomy 16), still followed today. Its discovery restores the belief that there is an authority above and beyond the whims and dictates of earthly rulers. Sadly, Josiah's reign came to an abrupt end when he became embroiled in military adventures and was killed in battle against the Egyptians.

IDEAS FOR EXPLORING FURTHER

The Written Word   Discuss the 'power of the pen'. What are the advantages of being able to write? (Cf. Story 34.) Why is an agreed spelling system required? When is speech more useful? Talk about time capsules as a way of showing future generations how we live today. What would pupils put in a time capsule and what would they write about themselves, family, school, friends to be read in a hundred years' time? Discuss the values/criteria used for choosing what to include/exclude. Perhaps actually bury a time capsule. (NC *English*)

Outward Signs   Should leaders set an example? Is it important for us to do so? Do actions speak louder than words? Put together an exhibition illustrating how one Jewish festival is celebrated. (See the Living Festivals series, RMEP.) Indicate some of the beliefs behind it. Consider the symbolism of food in celebrations/rituals.

34

In the Stocks and Down the Well

Jeremiah 19: 1 – 20: 6; 36; 38

The pot crashed to the ground. It smashed into a hundred pieces which flew across the courtyard. The crowd gasped.

'So says God. That is what is going to happen to this country. It will be smashed to pieces. We have been stupid. We have refused to follow God's ways. Now we shall become like that pot.'

The speaker was a tall, lean, young man with fiery eyes. His name was Jeremiah.

'Make way. Come on. Get out of the way. We'll soon deal with him.'

The crowd turned to see where the second voice came from. It was Pashur, the chief Temple officer with some of his guards. They pushed through the crowd, seized Jeremiah and dragged him away.

A few minutes later there came the sound of a cracking whip and screams. Some of the crowd saw Jeremiah again a few minutes later as they walked away. He was in the stocks round by the north side of the Temple. His back was bleeding. He was left there all night.

Next morning Pashur came back. 'All right,' he said to his men. 'Set him free.' He turned to Jeremiah. 'Perhaps that will teach you a lesson. Just you remember who I am, that's all. I am Pashur.'

Jeremiah glared at him. 'Pashur,' he spat. 'That means safety. I'll give you a more suitable name. What about "Total

142

Terror"? You'll know what terror is all about by the time the Babylonians get here. They'll soon destroy you like everything else.'

'Get out,' roared Pashur, 'before I have you whipped again.'

Jeremiah walked away. Pashur shook his head. He had a job to do but he couldn't help admiring Jeremiah. He might be a nuisance but he never gave up.

Jeremiah had not wanted to be a prophet. He liked a quiet country life. He just knew that God had made him speak out and there was nothing he could do about it. Somebody had to warn the people about the disaster which was coming. Now he couldn't speak in public any more. What was he going to do? He went to see his friend Baruch and told him what had happened.

'I can't go to the Temple any more,' Jeremiah said, 'but you can. Will you read my words for me?' He gave Baruch a scroll.

Baruch went off to the Temple courtyard. There were a lot of people there. Baruch climbed to the top of the steps, opened the scroll and began to read. The people stopped talking and started to listen. At the back of the crowd stood the son of a government minister. He listened for a few minutes, then hurried away. He told his father what was happening.

The minister sent soldiers to see what it was all about. They took the scroll from Baruch.

'I suppose you got this from Jeremiah,' said the soldiers.

'Yes,' replied Baruch.

'Go and hide,' said the officer in charge. 'The King will have to see this.'

The officer took the scroll to the King. It was winter. The King was sitting near a roaring fire. 'Read it,' he ordered. The officer started to read. When he had read one or two columns, the King called 'Stop!' Then he took out his knife, cut off the piece of scroll which had been read and threw it into the fire. 'Read on,' said the King.

The King went all through the scroll like that, listening and cutting and burning, until nothing was left of Jeremiah's scroll.

When it was finished the King said, 'Arrest both of them.'
But they could not be found. In hiding Jeremiah wrote out
his scroll again.

The Babylonians came as Jeremiah said they would. They
surrounded the city. Jeremiah came out of hiding. He went
back to the Temple and started talking. This is what he said:
'You're all frightened: I'm frightened. We can't beat the
Babylonians. We should surrender. Then at least we shall go
on living and so will our children.'
Before he could get any further a voice called out, 'Arrest
that man. He is a traitor.'
Jeremiah was taken away again. This time he was thrown
down an old well. It had no water in it but the bottom was all
mud and slime. He could not get out.
An African who worked at the palace heard Jeremiah's cries
for help. Very bravely he went to see the King himself. 'You
can't kill a prophet, sire,' he said. 'We may not like the
message but we all know he's a real prophet.'
The King nodded. 'All right. See what you can do,' he said.
The African got hold of some ropes and with the help of
three friends he managed to pull Jeremiah out of the well.
They took him back to the King.
The King looked at the filthy, muddy figure in front of him.
'If you're a prophet,' he said, 'tell me what to do.'
'Surrender,' replied Jeremiah straight away. 'It is the only
way to save God's people. Our children or grandchildren then
might be able to start again some day.'
And so it happened. Jeremiah was locked up in the guardhouse for his own safety. The gates were opened. The
Babylonians came and took the King, his courtiers and all the
important people. None of them was killed. They were
marched across the desert as prisoners to Babylon. Jeremiah
was left behind in Jerusalem. Later he fled to Egypt.
In Babylon the Jews were allowed to live in special camps,
but they were a thousand miles from home. The Exile had
begun.

144

NOTES

ABOUT THE STORY

Jeremiah is one of the greatest of the prophets and also typifies them. He is very reluctant to take on the role, preferring a life of peace and quiet in his own village of Anathoth, but feels compelled to speak out against what he sees as political and ungodly stupidity. His teaching methods are also startlingly modern. He uses actions and drama as well as words to make his points more vividly.

The Babylonians first besieged Jerusalem in 598 B.C.E. They deported some of the leading citizens but spared the Temple and, whilst exacting a heavy tribute, left Zedekiah, one of the sons of Josiah, on the throne. Judah and its religion remained intact. On the Babylonians' departure there were those who thought the best thing was to make alliances with the Egyptians. Jeremiah vehemently opposes this, knowing that the Babylonians will then come straight back with much more aggression. Judah can best survive by remaining neutral.

In the midst of all this Jeremiah makes a contribution to religious thinking which affects all of us. It is the idea that each individual can know God for him- or herself. In Jeremiah 31: 31–34 he writes of a 'new covenant' which will be written on 'people's hearts' rather than on tablets of stone for tribes and nations.

Such teaching adds to his reputation for treason. Emphasis on the individual's direct and personal relationship with God always challenges both priests and rulers. We can imagine that it is that idea which is written on the scroll destroyed within this story. Too late the inevitability of Jeremiah's political warning is accepted. The Babylonians are already at the gates.

The Jews are separated from their holy city, the Temple left to decay as they are marched across the desert to Babylon and exile. The year is 587 B.C.E. What happened to the northern tribes is now happening to Judah. It seems like the end of everything.

IDEAS FOR EXPLORING FURTHER

Patriotism   Does loyalty to a group mean never pointing out when it is going wrong? Think about sports teams. Are there some issues which go beyond loyalty to one's own group or country? Read the story of Edith Cavell, who was shot for nursing both British and German soldiers in the First World War. The Trafalgar Square monument bears her statement: 'Patriotism is not enough.' Is it important to think of oneself as a 'world citizen'?

Exile   Think about the journey. Consider the hardship and fears night and day, and reaction to the Jews' arrival in Babylon. Older children could consider traditions the Jews might have tried to maintain secretly: their prayers, their language, their story-telling, their festivals, their costumes, etc. How might the relationship with their captors have developed? Write an acrostic poem, a story or a play to reflect some of these ideas. (█ *English*)

145

Discuss the way Jews have become dispersed amongst many countries since being forced to leave Palestine by the Romans in 135 C.E. Use reference books to find some of the countries they went to and mark them on a world map. Try to indicate some of the contributions they made in each place. (NC *Geography:* AT 1) Note that the land they left gradually filled up with other people whom we now call Palestinians. It was not until 1947 that the Jews were once again able to form a nation settled in that land, which was then renamed Israel. What did the Palestinians think about this? Ask older pupils to collect and discuss newspaper accounts of the Israeli–Palestinian conflict.

35

Chariots of Fire and Valleys of Dry Bones

Ezekiel 1: 4–28; 37: 1–14

It seemed like the end of everything. The Jews were in Babylon, far from their own land. They had lost everything. Jerusalem, the Temple and the Ark of the Covenant were all destroyed. How could they worship God without a temple? How could God even hear them this far from home? Would they be prisoners for ever and ever? Would they just disappear like the ten tribes of the north had done?

There was one man who found answers to these questions. He was a priest called Ezekiel. He was also a prophet. Ezekiel dreamed strange dreams and saw colourful visions.

The first of Ezekiel's strange visions told how God was everywhere. The Jews did not have to go to Jerusalem to find him. He had found them in Babylon.

'I heard a mighty wind,' said Ezekiel. 'It came from the north out of a great cloud of flashing fire. From the middle of it came four strange creatures. They looked like men but when I looked closer I could see that each one had four faces. They could face north, south, east and west all at the same time.

'Together the four creatures moved across the sky on huge wings which touched one another. As they swept over me I could see that although the faces at the front were human faces, the others were of lions and oxen and eagles. They moved about in all directions and behind them the sky glowed with fire.

147

'Then I saw that behind each figure was a wheel of shining crystal. They were strange wheels – wheels within wheels, in fact. Like shining balls they could roll in any direction, backwards and forwards, to left or right.

'High above the wings and through the cloud there glowed a bright light. Suddenly I heard a noise, like a thundering waterfall. The moving creatures stopped and covered their faces with their wings.

'Out of the brightness of the sky I saw the outline of a throne. Upon the throne was a figure I could not look at. He shone like polished bronze. The whole sky was filled with light. It came down in a wide beam and touched the earth like a rainbow does. And then it all vanished – but not before I knew that God was there, God is here, God is everywhere.'

A long time later Ezekiel had another vision which he wrote down. This is how he described it:

'God took me in a dream and put me into a deep valley. It was full of dry bones. They were very old, dried white by the hot sun. God spoke to me. He said, "Do you think these bones can ever live again?"

'They looked very dead but I replied, "Only you know that, God."

'God spoke again, "Speak out," he said. "Talk to these bones. Tell them that I, God, will breathe life into them again. Tell them they will live. Tell them that I shall make them more than skeletons. I shall even put flesh on them and cover them with skin."

'So, I stood there and shouted out loud to those dead bones. Suddenly, there was a rattling and a shaking. Bones began to move across the ground. Foot bones joined up with leg bones. Leg bones joined hip bones. Soon whole skeletons grew before my eyes.

'Then, quick as lightning, they were covered with flesh and skin. But they were still dead bodies.

'God spoke again. "Speak out," he called. "Shout to the

148

force of life in the universe. Call for breath to the four winds. Order it into these bodies."

'I stood there and I shouted. I cried out to the sky and the land. And as I called the wind came from the north and the south, from the east and the west. It drove into those bodies and they came to life. They leapt to their feet, a great host of men and women. They lived again – a great nation.

'The dream faded. The vision disappeared.

'God spoke to me again. "Go to your people the Jews," he said. "Tell them what you have seen. Now they are dead bones but one day they will live again."

'I went and did as God had told me.'

NOTES

ABOUT THE STORY

It is a fact of history that from this point (587 B.C.E.) until 1947, a period of over 2500 years, the Jews never lived freely in their own country.

Ezekiel comes across as a strange and remote character. He is the only prophet who is known also to have been a priest. His prophecy is communicated through dreams which are both stark and strange. There is a wildness bordering on fanaticism about his whole image. As a result it is easy to laugh at him and to trivialize what he is saying. This has been done repeatedly down the centuries. And yet the images do not go away. Why?

The answer must lie in the importance of what we call 'vision'. The situation in which the Jews found themselves must have seemed completely and absolutely hopeless. Not only were they captive in a foreign land with no prospects of return but their whole faith and morale were shattered. Their God had proved impotent. He had been destroyed with the Temple in Jerusalem.

The first dream recorded here tells that this was not the case. The God of the Jews is infinitely mobile. His chariot has wheels within wheels. He is everywhere and anywhere.

The second dream is the great vision of hope. Judaism may have seemed as dead as a valley of dry bones but it would live again. This was to come true within sixty years but it was also to be a recurring truth. It is easy to make fun of 'dem bones, dem bones, dem dry bones' in the words of an old pop song, but the strength of Ezekiel's vision not only helped bring the Jews out of Babylon. It has helped them, as a community, to overcome Auschwitz too, as well as hundreds of other pogroms and persecutions down the centuries. The test of any belief or vision is whether or not it ultimately works.

149

IDEAS FOR EXPLORING FURTHER

Visions   How important is it to imagine what life *could* be like? It is said that 'nothing happens without first a dream'. Consider such things as: 'What I would like to be', 'What I would like my city/town/village to be like', 'What I would like the world to be like'. Older children could listen to Martin Luther King's great speech, 'I have a dream ...', and do work on similes and metaphors.

Hope   Consider people who might have to 'live in hope': hostages, prisoners, the aged, the poor, the sick, the homeless, etc. Make a class 'tree of hope' with each branch/leaf representing a group of people, and indicating their possible hopes for the future together with actions which might help them: prayer, visits, letters, gifts, listening, more just laws, etc.

36

Going Home

Psalm 137; Isaiah 40: 1–18

The Jews were still in Babylon. They were not shut up in prisons but they lived quite separately from the Babylonians. There was no Temple, so they found other ways of worshipping God. Instead of making sacrifices they sang hymns, read passages from the laws and the prophets and had sermons. They kept themselves to themselves and tried to keep alive the old ways. Jews married only other Jews. They kept Saturday as a special day – the sabbath, they called it – and they sang their own songs.

The Babylonians liked the music of the Jews. 'Come on,' they would say, 'sing us some of your Jewish songs. Let's hear you sing.'

The Jews liked singing to themselves. They didn't like singing to the Babylonians. So they made up a sad song for them. It was a lament, a song about why they couldn't sing their cheerful songs. It went like this:

> By the waters of Babylon
> We sat down and cried ·
> When we remembered Jerusalem.
> We hung our musical instruments
> On the branches of the willow trees.
> Our captors called for a song,
> Our tormentors asked for a tune.

151

'Sing us one of your Jerusalem songs,'
they cried.
How can we sing God's songs
In a foreign land?

Then one day there was a buzz of excitement through the Jewish camp. Men stood around in small groups. They spoke to one another almost in whispers.

'Have you heard what the new prophet is saying?'

'He says we must stop worrying. We will soon go back to Jerusalem.'

'How can that be possible? The Babylonians aren't going to set us free.'

'But Cyrus is coming.'

'Who's Cyrus?'

'He is King of the Persians. The Persians have beaten the Babylonians. Soon their army will be here. Then we shall be free.'

'So what? Being a prisoner of the Persians isn't going to be any better than being a prisoner of the Babylonians.'

'But the prophet says that Cyrus is God's messenger. He doesn't know it but God is using him to help us.'

'Let's wait and see. I don't understand half the things this prophet says. He speaks in poetry all the time.'

'Ssh! He's coming now. He's going to speak again.'

The men looked round. A crowd was beginning to form. At the front of it stood a lone figure. His hair and his beard were long. His eyes had a wild look in them. In one hand he held a staff. The other was raised in the air. The crowd fell silent.

The voice of the prophet rang out. His words were like music. It was as if the crowd were not there. He almost sang the words.

'Comfort, comfort my people,
says your God.
Speak to the heart of Jerusalem.
Tell her

152

Her slavery is over,
Her penalty paid.
She has suffered under God
Full measure for all her sins.

Listen – someone is calling.
Build God's road
Across the wastelands.
Clear a highway for our God
Across the desert.'

It happened just as the prophet had said. King Cyrus came to Babylon.

'Who are all these people?' he asked. 'They don't look like Babylonians.'

'No, Your Majesty, they aren't. Their grandparents were brought here from the city of Jerusalem about sixty years ago.'

'Then let them go home again,' ordered the King. 'Jerusalem is also part of my empire now. They will be happier there and I want no trouble.'

It was like the march from Egypt all over again. A few stayed behind in Babylon but most set off across the desert. Now they could sing their joyful songs. They would build the Temple again. They had learned their lesson. Now they would be a good and faithful people following the commandments of God. Nothing would go wrong this time.

But it did.

ABOUT THE STORY

The Exile lasted until 538 B.C.E., sixty years after the Babylonians had first captured Jerusalem. In that time the Jews learned to adjust to life in a foreign land and, at the same time, how to keep their identity. It was a lesson which was to become essential to their survival. Many of the features which today seem most to identify the Jewish people were probably first acquired during the Babylonian Exile.

Cut off from the Temple they developed a whole new way of worship. We might say the synagogue was invented at this time. Within it the Scriptures became far more important than burnt offerings. The people read again and again the accounts of their origins, began to revere the writings of the prophets, who had tried to keep them close to the original vision, and collected together their sacred songs or psalms.

Shabbat (the Sabbath) began to assume great importance. The yearly cycle of festivals remained and was developed but the weekly cycle, marked by a day when whole families and communities gave priority to being together, started to become supremely important. Mixed marriages became frowned upon.

The end of the Exile was heralded by one of Judaism's greatest poets and prophets. His name is unknown but his work was attached to the Book of Isaiah and now makes up chapters 40–55. As a result he is sometimes referred to as Deutero or Second Isaiah.

He did two things. First, he raised morale and gave back to the Jews their sense of dignity and high calling. Secondly, he created the image of that calling as being in the form of a suffering servant of God rather than as a superior and powerful nation. However, his picture of a dignified, marching return across the desert remained a poetic vision. As the next story shows, it was much more casual and chaotic than that and many chose not to return at all.

IDEAS FOR EXPLORING FURTHER

Special Days of the Week   Find out about the holy day of the week for different traditions. Discuss points in common.

Apartheid   Help older children to find out about and discuss the suffering of people forced to live apart in South Africa.

37

Cupbearer to the King

Nehemiah 1: 1 – 2: 10

Most of the Jews had left Babylon and gone back to Jerusalem. A few stayed behind. One of them was a man called Nehemiah. When Cyrus died a new king came to the throne. His name was Artaxerxes. Nehemiah became his trusted servant until one day something happened which changed his life. In the Bible Nehemiah tells his own story. It goes something like this.

I was cupbearer to King Artaxerxes. It was my job to serve his wine, and to taste it first. You never know who might want to poison a king.

We were in the city of Susa the day it all began. Some visitors came to the palace. I could see straight away that they were men of my own race. They had come from Jerusalem. I went over to talk to them.

'What's it like in Jerusalem?' I asked.

The reply took me by surprise. 'Terrible,' they said.

'Why?' I asked. 'What's happened?'

'Happened?' they repeated with a laugh. 'That's just the trouble. Nothing has happened.'

'But when you left here. . . .'

Before I could finish the sentence they said, 'When we left here everyone was singing. We dreamed about rebuilding Jerusalem. We were going to make the Temple beautiful again. Everything was going to be lovely.'

155

'But what went wrong?' I asked. 'Why hasn't the dream come true?'

The men laughed again. 'You should see it,' one of them said. 'You can't imagine the mess. Stones and rubbish everywhere. It's been a ruin for over seventy years. It's like a rubbish-dump. And anything worth having the Samaritans have stolen long ago. Those Samaritans really hate us Jews, you know.'

He stopped talking. He must have seen the look on my face. 'Cheer up,' he said. 'You're all right. It's better here. I wish we'd stayed.'

I had to go on duty. I tried to hide my feelings, but King Artaxerxes was no fool. He noticed everything. I passed him his wine as usual.

He held the goblet in his hand and looked at me. 'Nehemiah, are you ill?' he asked.

'Not at all, Your Majesty,' I replied.

'Then what are you looking so miserable about? Is there something wrong with the wine?'

'No, never!' I exclaimed. 'The wine is good. It is just that I feel very sad.'

'What is it? Tell me.'

It was an order. What could I do? I had to obey. I knew what I wanted to say but did I dare speak? The King could be moody. There was a long silence. Everyone was looking at me, waiting for me to speak. I breathed a quick prayer to God and said, 'Noble King, may you live for ever. I want to serve you cheerfully but I have just heard bad news.'

'What news?' asked the King.

'I am a Jew,' I replied, 'and I have just heard that our holy city of Jerusalem still lies in ruins. I thought it had been rebuilt, but I hear it is still nothing more than a pile of stones and burnt wood.'

The King said nothing. I looked up. His goblet was empty. Quickly I refilled it. He drank. Then he spoke again: 'Well, what do you want to do about it?'

It was the moment I had been frightened of. As soon as I had

156

heard the news I knew what I wanted to do. But I did not know if I dared ask the King. There was no going back now.

'Noble King,' I said, 'if I am in your favour, would you allow me to go and rebuild the city of Jerusalem?'

There was a silence. The King sipped his wine and looked at me. I waited. Suddenly he smiled and said, 'How long do you want to be away?'

I knew then that it was going to be all right. I did not know the answer to his question, but it did not matter.

Artaxerxes was very kind to me. He gave me a horse and ordered a squad of soldiers to go with me. He wrote some letters to the governors of the lands I had to travel through. Most important of all, he gave me a letter for Asaph. Asaph was keeper of the King's forests in Judah. The letter told him to let me have all the wood I needed for the job I had to do.

I was happy again as we rode out of Susa. Little did I know what lay ahead. Artaxerxes was a powerful king, but Jerusalem was a long way away. There were other people who did not want to see Jerusalem strong again. They would do almost anything to stop me.

NOTES

ABOUT THE STORY

The story of Nehemiah is dealt with here in two parts which can be run into one. As in the Bible the narrative is in the first person. This makes it at once unusual and appealing. There is a simple directness about Nehemiah's telling. Strangely, it rarely appears in children's anthologies.

The story contains very little of the lofty images and great vision of the poets and the prophets. It is very down to earth. Jerusalem is a shambles. Those who have made the return journey with high hopes have found the reality hard to take. During the sixty years of exile the city has been constantly pillaged by those living nearby. Such buildings as remain are in a bad state of repair. Worst of all the walls are in ruins so that there is no protection from raiders who aim to prevent any restoration.

Nehemiah is in a position of trust. He is cupbearer to the new king, Artaxerxes. It is his job to ensure that no one poisons the king; it is also his task to play something of the role of court jester, to keep the king in a good humour. To appear sad in the king's presence was itself to take a risk.

Nevertheless, Nehemiah's strategy works. The full story emerges and the request to return, with the king's full authority behind him, is granted. This is no small achievement. In modern terms permission to rebuild the walls was tantamount to being allowed to rearm.

What comes out of Nehemiah's simple prose is a picture of an ordinary man with some talents and great strength of character being prepared to take on a responsible task with integrity and realism. He possesses high ideals but he is also a person of action in the real world.

IDEAS FOR EXPLORING FURTHER

Damaged Sites (NC *History*: local study; CSU 2 – Fire of London; CSU 4 – Second World War) Look at pictures of bomb damage during the Second World War. Pupils may be able to bring some from home. List factors involved in rebuilding a town/city after a disaster. Discuss resources, labour, skills required, money, time. Look at before/after pictures of places like Coventry, Dresden, etc. Discuss how people from many countries (e.g. Jamaicans in the 1950s) came to Britain and contributed to getting the country back on its feet. Pupils could make a drawing of their home and mark all the things they would miss (memories, possessions, associations) if it were to be destroyed. Link up with NC *Geography*: AT 3 – natural disasters. See also Story 38.

38

Nehemiah and the Rebuilding of Jerusalem

Nehemiah 2: 11 – 4: 22

We rode up the hill to Jerusalem. Our horses were glad to stop. I looked around. What a sight met my eyes. So this was the city I had waited so long to see.

The officer of the bodyguard rode across to me. 'Is this what your people call the greatest city on earth?' he asked. 'Have we travelled all this way to look at this ruin?'

I could see what he meant. There was nothing but piles of stones with weeds growing between them.

'It was great once,' I replied. 'It will be great again. That is why I have come.'

The officer shrugged his shoulders but said nothing. He had his orders from King Artaxerxes. That was enough. He would do as I said. He was not a Jew. He could never understand what this place meant to my people.

From the ruins people began to appear. It seemed that they were living in caves and shacks in the middle of the rubble. I looked across at the soldiers with me.

'Tell no one why we are here,' I ordered. 'Tonight we will look more carefully at what has to be done.'

That night the moon was very bright. I took three men and we made our way through the deserted city. Our horses picked their way over the stones. I rode outside the old walls to see if I could make out where the gates had been. It was no good. I had to give up. When I tried to go down the hill to where the King's Pool and the Fountain Gate should have been, there was so much rubbish that my horse could not even find spaces large enough for his hoofs. What the Babylonians had not destroyed the Samaritans had knocked over.

Next day I called a meeting. News of our coming had spread quickly and people came out from many places to see what we wanted.

I stood up and said, 'We are going to rebuild the city.'

They looked at one another. I could see that they thought I was mad. It seemed an impossible task.

I started to tell them my plan. Then I asked the crowd to follow me. We began to walk by the side of the ruined wall. I turned to the man next to me. His name was Eliashib and he had been made High Priest.

'Here you are,' I said, 'this is where the old Sheep Gate stood. Get your priests together and get on and rebuild that. Don't bother what anyone else is doing. If we think of the whole city we shall give up. Just think about your little piece.'

I left Eliashib and the priests and walked on. When I stopped again I looked back and gave that section to a group of men who came from Jericho. And so we went on right round the city. It was important to get the walls up first. Then we could take our time on the buildings inside.

Everyone was more cheerful now. The work began. Gateposts began to go up. People swarmed everywhere like ants. I rode around from place to place.

Soon, I thought, other people will notice. The Samaritans especially – what will they do? I knew one or two people had gone to tell Sanballat, the Samaritans' leader, what was happening. But he did not come. 'I'll send a fox,' he had said. 'It will jump over the walls. You'll never build them again like they were before.'

He was wrong. The work went well. The walls started to get high. One day a man rushed up to me in a great hurry. He had just come back from Samaria. 'Sanballat's coming,' he gasped. 'He says he's going to come and kill a few of the workmen. Then the rest will run away. You've got to make

160

them all work faster and get the walls finished before he comes.'

I thought for a moment. Then I said, 'No, we will work more slowly. Tell the men to work with one hand only. The other must hold a sword at all times. A boy with a trumpet will ride alongside me. If the Samaritans come I will ride to where the fighting is. When the trumpet sounds everyone will drop his tools and come running.'

Sanballat must have heard of my plan. He never came. Instead he tried another trick. He sent a messenger to ask me to meet him secretly. As if I would fall for that! Then he got really angry. He said he would tell King Artaxerxes that I was making myself into a king. Let him. I knew the King better than he did. They really hate us, these Samaritans. I don't know if we can ever be friendly after this.

Now it is done. The walls are up; the gates are working. We can go inside and start to rebuild houses and the Temple. Then we can hold the biggest celebration that Jerusalem has seen since David brought the Ark of the Covenant here hundreds of years ago.

NOTES

ABOUT THE STORY

The story continues in Jerusalem itself. It was the Jews, those living in and immediately around Jerusalem, who had been deported sixty years before. The 'people of the land', those who lived nearby and were closely related, had been the first to take advantage. Their centre was the city of Samaria (just to the north of modern Nablus). We have here a continuation of, and more reasons for, the enmity between Jews and Samaritans which had begun at the time of the Division of the Kingdom and was to continue for hundreds of years. Some would suggest that it has not yet fully ended.

Far from welcoming back their neighbours the Samaritans do everything to prevent their return. It was they who had pillaged Jerusalem; it is they now who use every trick of intimidation to stop the rebuilding.

Nehemiah's response is to keep a cool head and not to reply in kind. He does not attack. His courage consists of refusing to go away. When his builders are threatened with physical violence he slows down the work so that attention can be given to self-defence but he does not stop or hurry.

IDEAS FOR EXPLORING FURTHER

Cooperation   Discuss how, with each group contributing a section, the reconstruction of the walls was achieved. Collect images of Jerusalem from different times/places. Consider what people are trying to say about Jerusalem through the way they present the city. As a class, plan, sketch then make a large collage of Jerusalem with everyone contributing something towards it. Alternatively, make a large clay model of the city. Discuss other tasks which people achieve by working together: building a house, making a road, getting aid to disaster areas, running a business. Play team games and draw out the value of team spirit. (Cf. Story 17.)

39

Too Many Rules

The Book of Ezra

Once again the city of Jerusalem stood proudly on the highest hill. Its white stone walls shone in the hot sun. In the middle of the city the Temple rose up against the blue sky. Nehemiah had done his job well.

Now another traveller came to Jerusalem from Babylon. He too felt that he had a job to do, but it was a very different task. Ezra was a priest and he came to Jerusalem with a book of rules.

Nehemiah had rebuilt the city because for all the Jews it was a holy place. Ezra was determined to make sure that it really was holy.

First he went to the Temple. There he counted up all the treasures, the gold candlesticks, the ornaments, the altar coverings and the rich curtains. They were all there. Everything had been restored.

Next day he called a big meeting. The people gathered together in Water Gate Square. It was early in the morning. Ezra stood up on a wooden platform which had been specially made. In his hands he held a large scroll. He held it up. 'This is the new law,' he said. 'If we are to be pure Jews we must keep all these rules.'

He started to read. His voice droned on and on. It was a very long scroll. The sun got higher and higher in the sky. The crowd began to get a bit fidgety. It was very, very boring and not everybody was listening.

Suddenly in the crowd a woman began to sob. 'I can't do it.

I can't do it,' she called out. 'There's too much. I can't keep all those rules. I shan't even be able to remember them all.'

'Quiet!' snapped Ezra. 'This is a holy day. Pull yourself together. We can't have you making a noise like that.'

The woman sobbed quietly to herself.

'He's too strict,' someone whispered in the crowd. People nodded but they said nothing. They were frightened of this priest.

Ezra went on reading. It was midday before he finished. The crowd broke up straight away. People walked off silently, talking only in whispers.

'That woman was right,' said one man. 'No one can keep all those rules.'

'I don't think she was a pure Jew, that's the trouble,' said his friend. 'There are people here now from all over the world. He seemed to be saying that only pure Jews could stay here.'

'Yes, we are going to hear more about that.'

He was right. A few days later Ezra called another meeting. This time he had another scroll. It contained all the names of the people whose families had been in Babylon and had never mixed with foreigners. A lot of people's names were missing.

In his strictest voice Ezra said, 'I have heard that some men here are still thinking of marrying foreign women – women from families that stayed behind here or in Samaria when the real Jews were taken to Babylon. It won't do. We made mistakes before. Now we are going to be pure. All foreigners have got to go – now! Any wife who has foreign blood in her will have to be divorced.'

There were gasps of 'No! No!' all through the crowd. Women began to cry. A few people cheered but many others said, 'This can't be what God wants.'

There were protests, but it was no good. A few days later a sad procession of women and children left Jerusalem. They were being forced to go back to the countries that their grandparents and their great grandparents had once come from. Everyone was crying. A few men went too. They would rather leave Jerusalem than their families.

164

Those who stayed were all pure Jews. But not all of them were happy. God had rescued them from Babylon. But what for? Was Ezra right? Were they saved so that they could become pure and special? Or were they saved so that they could go out and mix with the rest of the world to tell everybody about their god? A big argument started. It has been going on ever since.

NOTES

ABOUT THE STORY

Both Ezra and Nehemiah were dedicated to restoring Judaism and to the idea of a holy people but their approaches could hardly have been more different. In their contrast we see what was destined to become the great divide between those who see religion as a freedom-giving experience, open to everyone (the universalists), and those who see it as making themselves special and privileged, superior to other people (the particularists). It is a divide which is still with us and can be seen in modern Israel and many other places.

Ezra is thought to have come to Jerusalem in about 444 B.C.E. The city had been rebuilt thanks to Nehemiah, whose leadership had been effective but unassuming and appears to have been characterized by a desire to serve. Nehemiah seems to have been prepared to work with anyone who would join him in the task of restoring the city as a symbol of the presence of Israel's God in the world.

Ezra's idea of holiness could not have been more different. He demanded purity, including racial purity. He saw his mission as that of cutting out all alien elements which, in his eyes, contaminated the true Israel. He demanded a return to formal ritualism and, most severe of all, the expulsion from the city of all who could not prove unblemished Jewish ancestry. These were mainly if not entirely women – foreign wives. The true Jews were those who had survived the Exile (the names of those families who had gone into Exile were known) and had not intermarried while in Babylon. The rule book and the genealogical records were supreme. Those who did not conform were forced to leave. Families were broken up.

The story of Ezra represents one extreme view of what it means to be a 'chosen people', namely a 'pure' race. It is a concept from which the Jews themselves have suffered many times since. And yet is the opposite attainable or desirable? How important is family and country to any form of self-identity? Can there be pride in one's roots and heritage without any accompanying feelings of exclusiveness and superiority?

165

IDEAS FOR EXPLORING FURTHER

Interpreting the Rules Do different people interpret rules in the same way? Discuss the school rules. What behaviour counts as breaking/keeping them? Are there any which often cause arguments? When might it be right to break a rule (e.g. by running instead of walking)? Do similar issues arise with rules in the Bible and other sacred writings (e.g. 'Do not steal')? Discuss how believers seek answers to questions about how God wants them to behave. Help pupils to raise questions themselves and discuss the difficulty of finding firm answers. Discuss how religious traditions show where people have sought answers before, through prayer, discussion, reading, etc. Pursue pupils' questions with illustrations from different traditions to provide food for thought. (Cf. *Exploring Questions*, CEM.)

Making Laws Discuss with older children why the law of the land exists. What criteria should be used for drawing up laws? Can we think of all people as part of God's family? (Cf. Story 41.) Think about human rights. (NC *Citizenship*; see also Stories 11 and 12.) What could be the consequences of disobeying the law for oneself and others? Is it right to make laws which distress people, split families or favour one group more than another? Would it ever be right to rebel and to disobey the law? Consider Robin Hood, places where religious freedom is suppressed, or where laws are/have been harsh or cruel. Should laws be inflexible? (Cf. Story 44.) Did Ezra confuse being pure on the inside and being racially pure? Which is more important and why? Discuss the proposition 'It is good to have some rules; it is bad to have too many.'

40

A Faithful Foreigner

The Book of Ruth

There were a lot of unhappy people in Jerusalem. All the men who had married foreign wives had had to send them away. They could not believe that that was what God really wanted.

One day there was great excitement. Somebody had written a story. It was all about a foreign wife who had lived a long time ago. Her name was Ruth and she had been the great grandmother of David, who had become the greatest king Israel had ever had. Everyone knew that the story was true, but now that foreign wives had been sent away the story suddenly had a lot more meaning. This is the story of Ruth, the faithful foreigner.

Long, long ago in the days of Gideon there was a terrible famine in the land. A man from Bethlehem, called Elimelech, took his wife Naomi and their two sons and travelled to the land of Moab. They found food there and the family stayed and settled down.

The two sons grew up and married girls from Moabite families. Elimelech died and then quite suddenly both of his sons died as well.

Naomi did not know what to do. She was a widow in a foreign land. There was no one to look after her except the wives of her two sons. They were widows too but they were not even of the same race as Naomi.

Naomi decided she would have to go home to Israel. She went to see the wives of her dead sons.

'I shall go home,' she said. 'You must leave me and go back to your own fathers' houses.'

Orpah, one of the wives, sadly agreed. She packed her things, kissed Naomi and set off at once. Ruth, the other wife, did nothing. Naomi started to get ready for her own journey. She realized that Ruth was still there.

'Off you go, Ruth,' she said. 'It will be better for you to stay here in your own country.'

'Please don't make me stay,' replied Ruth. 'Wherever you go, I shall go. Wherever you live, I shall live. Your god shall become my god.'

'But when I die,' answered Naomi, 'you will be worse off than I am now. You will be a stranger in a foreign land with no one to look after you.'

Ruth would not give in. She said again, 'Wherever you go, I shall go. Wherever you live, I shall live. Your god shall become my god. Wherever you die, I shall die.'

The two women set off. It was a long, hard journey, but after many days of walking they finally came to Bethlehem.

It was early summer. The barley was being gathered. It was the custom in Israel to let the poor people come into the fields after the harvesters and gather the loose grains from the ground. This was called gleaning.

Naomi and Ruth had little to eat so one morning Ruth went into the fields to glean. It was hard work; it meant being bent double all day long.

The field belonged to a farmer called Boaz who was a distant relation of Naomi. He noticed Ruth. 'Who is that young woman?' he asked.

'That is Ruth, the daughter-in-law of Naomi,' came the answer. 'She shouldn't be gleaning really. She's a foreigner.'

Boaz nodded. He had heard about Ruth and the way she helped Naomi. He allowed her to stay and even to eat and drink with the other gleaners. That surprised Ruth because the

Jews were very strict. They would not eat and drink with foreigners.

Ruth was still an attractive young woman. Boaz was a rich farmer but he had no wife. Although she was a foreigner he liked Ruth more and more and in the end he married her. Together they were able to look after Naomi.

Ruth and Boaz had children. Their first son was called Obed. When Obed grew up he had a son as well. His name was Jesse. In the course of time Jesse grew up, married and had many sons. One of them was David who became the great King of Israel. It was David who captured Jerusalem and brought the Ark there. Jerusalem became the holy city of the Jews because of him.

Now Ezra had sent away all the foreign wives. If Boaz had sent Ruth away, David would never have been born and Jerusalem would not have been a holy city.

NOTES

ABOUT THE STORY

This story and the next were once among the best-known stories in the Bible but their context is less well known and is important. We know now that they were written about the time of Ezra and represent the fight back by unknown writers against the repression of the particularists.

The story of Ruth was an old story, set way back in the period of the Judges. The timing of its revival makes a powerful point. The Jews had survived the traumatic experience of the Exile. They still existed as a people set apart by their belief in God but they were striving to recover their confidence and their real identity. Calls to purify the race were a part of that struggle.

One period of Jewish history stood out by now as the Golden Age. That was the period of King David, when Israel was strong, sure of herself and faithful, led by a monarch who was also a man of God. The story of Ruth is beautiful and very meaningful in its own right but, seen in this context, there is a powerful 'kick in the tail'. It comes in the form of a simple, short genealogical table. Not only was this most faithful and loyal daughter-in-law a foreigner, not only did she prove to be religiously true to Israel's God but she was to become the great grandmother of David. The great monarch of the Golden Age was himself of mixed blood. The implication is strong. If Ezra's laws had been in force Ruth would have been driven out and David would never have been born a Jew.

Driven from her homeland by famine Naomi finds herself widowed and alone. Her sons had married what to her are foreign women but they too are now widows. It is the nightmare of all poor emigrants – to be alone without family in an alien society. Ruth, one of the daughters-in-law, meets the situation head on with the eloquent lines 'Wherever you go, I will go. Wherever you live, I will live. Your people shall be my people and your god my god.' (Ruth 1: 16)

But it is one thing, as the Ezra episode shows, to declare that 'your people shall be my people' and quite another for that people to recognize Ruth as 'one of us'. It is Boaz who redeems that situation by marrying her. Again, under Ezra the marriage would not have been permitted.

Finally, the old, humanitarian custom of gleaning appears in this story. Fallen grapes, the borders of cornfields and the loose wheat which fell during harvesting were to be left for the landless poor and the stranger (see the 'social-security' law in Leviticus 19: 9).

IDEAS FOR EXPLORING FURTHER

'Foreigners'   Look at the family tree of the British royal family. Find out the countries of origin of some of its members. Record them on a map. How many nationalities have contributed to the blood of Prince Charles? (Cf. Stories 10, 11, 18, 39, 41.)

Barriers   Brainstorm for barriers such as race, language, age, handicap. Who is it most difficult to make friends with? Why? Is it anyone's fault? Take one barrier and work in groups to decide how that barrier might be overcome. Read the story of Helen Keller (see *Helen*, by G. Hanks, Faith in Action series, RMEP) and draw out the factors required to help Helen overcome her handicaps. (See also *Exploring a Theme: Barriers*, CEM.)

Home and Family   (Cf. Story 3.) Compare family life in different localities. Consider the feelings of people who cannot afford a solid roof over their heads, and how housing problems are often related to poverty. (NC *Geography*: AT 2)

41

Jonah and the Big Fish

The Book of Jonah

The Jews should have been happy. The Babylonians who had swallowed them up had been forced to let them go free. Now they were back in their own land. But they weren't happy at all. They began to argue with one another.

'We are special,' said some of the Jews. 'We were rescued because we are God's people and we must be pure. We mustn't mix with other people.'

'That's wrong,' said others. 'Just because we are God's people shouldn't make us all high and mighty. We should mix with everybody and tell them about God.' But they weren't listened to. Most Jews would have nothing to do with foreigners.

Then one day a story appeared. No one knows who wrote it. It was all about a man called Jonah. When people first read it they all knew that Jonah was really all the Jews. His adventures were really what happened to them, and when they laughed at him because he was stupid, they were laughing at themselves. This sort of story with a meaning we call a parable. This is the parable of Jonah and the big fish.

One day God said to Jonah, 'Jonah, I want you to go across the desert to a big city called Nineveh. When you get there, tell all the people about me.'

Jonah said, 'Yes, God,' but he thought to himself, Nineveh is a terrible place. The people there have a lot of dirty habits.

They are rough and nasty. I don't like them. I'm not going there. I'll run away where God won't find me.

Jonah packed his bags, went down to the harbour and bought a ticket for a boat. He was going to go as far from Nineveh as he could get.

The boat sailed away on a calm sea. But that night a terrible storm blew up. The ship was tossed up and down like a cork. The sailors thought they were going to drown.

The captain could not understand it. He had never seen a storm like it before. What had caused it? He called the crew together. 'There's something funny about this storm,' he said. 'It seems to be just near our ship. What's different about us?'

Everyone turned and looked at Jonah.

'Oh, dear,' cried Jonah, 'it's all my fault. I came on board to run away from God but I think he's seen me. There's only one way to save the ship. You must throw me overboard.'

'We can't do that,' said the sailors. They quite liked poor Jonah even though he was a bit stupid.

It was only a small boat so the sailors got out the oars and tried to row back to the shore. But every time they turned, the wind moved in front of them and blew them back. The boat started to fill with water.

'You will have to throw me in,' shouted Jonah above the noise of the wind. 'It's the only way.'

The crew stopped rowing. Sadly they agreed. They picked up Jonah, said a quick prayer to ask God to forgive them, and dropped him into the sea. Straight away the wind stopped. The sea went calm and the boat sailed peacefully away.

Jonah was in the water a long way from the shore. That was bad enough, but suddenly the water underneath him moved. A huge black fish came to the surface right next to him. It looked at him through small beady eyes and opened its mouth. It was the size of a cave. Jonah screamed and tried to swim away, but it was no good. With one gulp the fish swallowed Jonah.

Jonah felt himself sliding down the long, dark, slippery tunnel of the fish's throat. He landed with a bump on the slimy

172

bottom of the stomach of the fish. It was pitch dark. Jonah was very frightened. 'I'm a fool,' he said. 'Fancy thinking I could run away from God as easily as that. I'm one of his people. I should have done what he said.' Then he thought, I wonder if it's too late even now. I bet God can hear me even from here. So he prayed as he'd never prayed before. 'God,' said Jonah, 'if you get me out of this mess I'll do anything you ask.'

For three days and three nights Jonah prayed. Nothing happened. He had just about given up hope when, suddenly, he felt the fish give a huge gulp. Jonah found himself being sucked up the tunnel of the fish's throat. Then he was flying through the air out of the darkness into bright sunlight. He fell with a bump on to something soft and yellow. He was on a beach.

Jonah stood up. Straight away God spoke to him. 'Now will you do as I say and go to Nineveh?'

Jonah nodded and went.

For days he tramped across the hot desert until he came to the city. It was as bad as he had always imagined it would be. The city was hot and dusty; the people were mean and un-friendly. Jonah hated it. But he had made a promise and he had to keep it. He went around telling everybody about the God of the Jews. To his surprise people listened. Then one day the King of Nineveh sent for him.

When the King heard what Jonah had to say he issued a decree. It said that all the people of Nineveh would accept the God of the Jews and change their way of living.

Jonah should have been pleased. He wasn't. He was very angry. He did not like the people of Nineveh. Secretly he had been hoping that they would not listen to him. Then God could have punished them. Jonah would have enjoyed that. Now it looked as if God would love them as much as he loved the Jews. Jonah would have to treat them as if they were part of his own family. He couldn't bear even the thought of it.

Jonah went out of the city, sat down in the shade and sulked. He sulked until he fell asleep. The plant he sheltered under was a desert plant like a huge piece of rhubarb. It grew quickly and

173

died quickly. When he woke up Jonah found that he was sitting in the hot sun. The plant had withered away. He felt very miserable.

Jonah beat the ground with his fist. 'I want to die,' he shouted.

'What for?' asked God. 'Why are you so unhappy?'

'I've got every right to be,' replied Jonah. 'It's a cruel world. I have to put up with all those horrible people from Nineveh. Then when I come out here to enjoy a bit of peace and quiet, what happens? I find a beautiful plant and within a few hours it's dead. The world is a horrible place.'

'Aren't people funny?' said God to Jonah. 'You ought to be pleased when thousands of bad people become good. You're more worried about a plant than about them. Why do people love things more than other people? You all belong to me. Why can't you live like one big family?'

Jonah had no answer. He went home to think about it.

ABOUT THE STORY

As in the case of the Book of Ruth we know that the Book of Jonah was written just over three hundred years before the birth of Jesus of Nazareth. Although there had been a prophet called Jonah five hundred years or so before, there can be little doubt that no Jew coming across this story in the aftermath of the Ezra affair would have had the slightest doubt what it was all about.

Jonah is Israel, the big fish is Babylon and the time during which one was swallowed up by the other is the sixty-year period of the Exile. Note that there is no mention of a whale! The Hebrew term *dag gadol* means literally 'a big fish'. The Greek *ketos* can be translated as 'whale', and has been in Matthew 9: 24, but it normally has more general meanings, appearing in dictionaries as 'a huge fish, sea monster', etc.

The Jonah story is a delightful compression of Israel's history and seeks to answer the theological question 'What does Israel exist for?' The answer offered is the universalist answer – to bring knowledge of and belief in Israel's God to the whole world. Nineveh is the Gentile world. No city 'three days' journey in breadth' (i.e. larger than present-day London) ever existed in the ancient world.

Jonah's (Israel's) reaction to being called to serve and to save the Gentile world is to run away from God. Disaster follows, for which he acknowledges responsibility. He pays the price of being swallowed up but is regurgitated. For what reason? To hear the command again. This time he does as he is told but with a very bad grace. He still sees himself as superior to Nineveh and he wants its destruction rather than its salvation. He has still failed to understand the real nature of the God he professes to worship, which is one of universal love and care. Jonah wants privilege and prefers to keep himself pure. Israel has not yet learned her lesson.

IDEAS FOR EXPLORING FURTHER

A Message for All People   (Cf. Stories 10, 11, 12, 18, 39, 40.) Discuss the message of universal love and care that God wanted Jonah to deliver to all nations. Talk about the purpose of greetings cards used to celebrate different festivals. What images/messages do they carry? What are the cards reminding people about? Design a card or artefact to illustrate love and concern for all people everywhere. What shape will it be? What materials, symbols and images will be used? Who will receive it? (NC *Technology; English*)

Messages in Stories and Visions   Make links with stories from Aesop's fables; see also Stories 35, 45, 48. Perhaps use the hyena story from the Introduction. Look back through stories read during the past day/week/month and ask of each one, 'Is it true?'; 'Does it contain truth?'

175

42

A Revolution over a Pig

1 Maccabees 1; 2
*(The Books of Maccabees are part of the Apocrypha which is not
included in all editions of the Bible.)*

'The Greeks are coming. Run!'

The shout could be heard all through the village. Women
ran out into the street, picked up their small children and
rushed indoors.

Led by an officer the small group of Greek soldiers marched
into the village street. They went straight to the house of the
village priest. They stopped outside.

Behind the closed door the old priest Mattathias waited. His
five grown-up sons were in the room with him. They had
known for a long time what was going to happen. Now they
were ready.

The Greeks had conquered the Persians. That had been all
right. Alexander the Great had left the Jews alone. But now
there were other Greeks who had different ideas. They were
determined to make all the world just like Greece. This man
Antiochus was the worst. He was Governor of Judah. Now he
had decided to destroy the religion of the Jews.

Here in the village of Modin they had found it hard to
believe the news. Away in Jerusalem, it was said, the Greeks
had actually sacrificed pigs on the sacred altar in the Temple.
Pigs! Mattathias shuddered at the thought. It was the biggest
insult anyone could make to a Jew. No Jew would ever eat
pork. To them the pig was an unclean animal. Now the
Greeks were here in the village.

Mattathias knew what he was going to do. He took a

firm grip on the dagger which was hidden by his cloak and waited.

There was a hammering on the door. The old priest opened it. There stood the Greek officer, sword in hand. Behind him stood his soldiers.

'Are you the priest of this village?' asked the officer.

'I am,' replied Mattathias.

'Then you know why we are here.'

The old priest nodded.

'It is by order of Antiochus that you shall sacrifice a pig on the altar at the shrine which is in this village.'

'Never! I will die first.' His voice shook with anger.

The Greek officer held his sword more tightly. These Jews, he thought to himself. They are so obstinate. It was no use arguing. He spoke sharply. 'Very well,' he said. 'If you won't, there are others who will. But you are under arrest. You will come with us and watch the ceremony. Then you will be taken back to Jerusalem.' He turned to his men. 'Bring them along,' he said.

At the shrine a large crowd of people had gathered. Mattathias and his sons were pushed to the front. The soldiers stood guard at the back of the crowd.

The officer turned to Mattathias. 'One last chance,' he said. 'Will you make the sacrifice? There are many of your fellow Jews who are on our side, you know.'

Mattathias spoke up so that all the crowd could hear him. 'If the whole world has gone to your side,' he declared, 'I and my sons and my whole family will keep God's covenant.'

The Greek officer made a signal. Another Jew stepped forward. He got ready to perform the ceremony. As he moved towards the altar Mattathias suddenly leapt forward. He raised his arm. The dagger flashed in the sunlight and the Jew screamed as the old priest drove it into his back. The officer, sword in hand, jumped forward. Mattathias was too quick for him. He turned. The dagger flashed again in the sun and the officer fell dead to the ground.

Screams and shouts broke out all around. People began to

run. The rest of the Greek soldiers were pushed over in the panic. Above it all came the voice of Mattathias: 'Follow me, all those who would keep God's covenant.'

With his five sons and a small group of men Mattathias made his way up into the hills. When news got back to Antiochus he would send many soldiers out to look for them. He would try to kill them all. First, though, he had to find them. In the wilderness there were many hiding-places. Antiochus and his Greeks were strangers in the land. Mattathias and his freedom fighters knew every inch of the mountains and the valleys. A revolution had begun.

NOTES

ABOUT THE STORY

The biblical books which modern scholars now know were written shortly before the Christian era are often less well understood than the early patriarchal narratives. This is because the stories which give the historical background are not contained within the Bible at all, but rather in the collection of books called the Apocrypha. This is a pity because not only does a vital part of the whole story get lost but some books which are in the Bible, particularly the Book of Daniel, are separated from their proper background. This is also the period which saw the rise of such groups as the Pharisees, Sadducees and Essenes.

In 334 B.C.E. Alexander the Great crossed the Hellespont and began his speedy conquest of the Persian Empire, which included Judah. His intention was to establish Greek culture wherever he went but he died in 323 B.C.E. without a successor. His generals fought amongst themselves and the Greek Empire became divided. Ptolemy gained control in Egypt, Seleucid Antiochus in Syria. Their respective dynasties fought over the ground in between, including Palestine. In 198 B.C.E. the Seleucids eventually gained control under Antiochus III.

It was his son Antiochus IV (calling himself Antiochus Epiphanes – 'God made manifest') who lost patience with the Jews and decided to stamp out their religion. In 168 B.C.E. he desecrated the Temple by building a pagan altar there and sacrificing pigs as the ultimate offence. He made it punishable by death for any Jew to possess a copy of the Torah (the first five books of the Bible), observe the Sabbath or circumcise male children. Revolt was inevitable. It began in the village of Modin when Antiochus' troops were sent to test Jewish loyalty. Heavily outnumbered the rebels took to the hills and under Judas Maccabeus (the Hammerer) led what we would now call a successful guerilla campaign. The full story is told in the four Books of Maccabees.

IDEAS FOR EXPLORING FURTHER

The Greeks   Relate this story to a project on Ancient Greece (█NC█ *History*: CSU 5). Find out as much as possible about Greek culture and language. In particular, explore the life story of Alexander the Great and read some Greek myths and legends. Do any of these carry familiar messages?

Chanukah   The Jewish festival of Chanukah celebrates every autumn the eventual triumph of Judas Maccabeus over Antiochus, and the return of the Temple to Jewish worship. (Cf. Stories 24, 25, 35, 37, 38.) Consider other festivals of light which symbolize hope and joy. (See Living Festivals series, RMEP.)

Music   Play part of Handel's oratorio 'Judas Maccabeus'. Discuss how the music represents ideas and emotions. Ask the children to use untuned percussion (or tuned percussion and other instruments) to compose short pieces of music which illustrate the different aspects of the story.

43

A Raging Furnace of Fire

1 Maccabees 3; Daniel 3

Fighting against the Greeks was hard. The Jews had only a small group of men. They lived in the hills and moved from place to place so that the Greeks could not find them.

Their leader was Judas, one of the sons of the old priest Mattathias who had started the revolution. Judas had a nickname. His men called him Maccabeus, which meant 'The Hammerer'. Although they were so few and the Greek army was so big, they kept hitting hard like a hammer. At night Judas would lead his men down from the hills. They would attack quickly and quietly and then run away again back into the hills.

At other times they would stay near the caves where they lived. Then they would gather round a camp-fire and sing and talk. They also listened to stories, stories of the great heroes of the past. The Greeks wanted to destroy their religion. Other people had tried to do that before. They had always failed because the Jews had been ready to die for what they believed in. There had been men like Shadrach, Meshach and Abednigo. How they loved to hear that story.

Long, long ago when the Jews were captives in Babylon, King Nebuchadnezzar made a great golden image. It was thirty metres high and three metres wide.

Nebuchadnezzar called together all his governors, mayors, police chiefs and magistrates. The Royal Herald made a

180

speech. He said, 'People of all nations. When the trumpet sounds you are to fall down and worship the image set up by King Nebuchadnezzar. If anyone refuses, he will be put to death by being thrown into a raging furnace of fire.'

The trumpet sounded. Everyone fell flat on their faces in front of the great idol. Only three people remained standing. They were three Jews called Shadrach, Meshach and Abednigo. They were reported to the King. He sent for them.

Shadrach, Meshach and Abednigo were brought to the palace. They stood in front of the King.

'Is it true,' asked Nebuchadnezzar, 'that you refuse to obey my commands? I am told you do not worship the golden image I have set up. You are good men and you have served me well in the past, but I must be obeyed. When the trumpet sounds you must bow down like everyone else or you will be thrown in the fire.'

The three men replied together. 'O Nebuchadnezzar,' they said, 'we will obey you in many things, but this is no time for words. Our God is greater than any king, even you. If he wants to he can rescue us from your furnace. But even if he doesn't we still won't worship an idol.'

Nebuchadnezzar blazed with anger. No one had ever spoken to him like that before. He screamed at his soldiers: 'Make the furnace seven times hotter than normal. Then throw these three into it.'

The King went off to watch from a safe distance. The furnace roared at the bottom of the pit. More and more wood was thrown on. The flames leapt higher and higher. Those watching had to move farther and farther back. From the top of the slope they could see right down into the furnace. In the middle it was white hot.

'Throw them in,' commanded the King.

The soldiers tied the hands of Shadrach, Meshach and Abednigo. Then they ran them towards the edge of the furnace and pushed them in. It was so hot that most of the soldiers could not get back. They were scorched to death on the edge of the pit.

Nebuchadnezzar watched it all. Suddenly he sat up. 'How many men did you throw in?' he called to his men.

'Three, Your Majesty,' came the reply.

'But there are four men down there – and look, they are walking around! That fourth one doesn't look human. He looks like an angel.'

Nebuchadnezzar went as near as he could to the furnace. He called out, 'Shadrach, Meshach and Abednigo. Come out of the furnace. I can see that your God has rescued you.'

The three Jews climbed out of the pit. The fire had not touched them. Even their clothes and their hair were not burnt.

'I hereby issue a new decree,' declared Nebuchadnezzar. 'Anyone who says anything against the God of Shadrach, Meshach and Abednigo shall be torn limb from limb and his house shall be knocked to the ground.'

The Babylonians who had reported the three Jews to Nebuchadnezzar shook with fear and hurried away. They could not fight against the God of the Jews.

As Judas the Hammerer and his men listened to this story it made them feel more brave and determined. They too had to be ready to die for their faith, but they knew that in the end no one could defeat their God.

ABOUT THE STORY

This and the following two narratives are stories within stories. We can say with a high degree of certainty that the Book of Daniel was written between 168 and 164 B.C.E., that is, during the Maccabean rebellion. It consists of stories set in Babylon during the long and difficult years of exile three centuries earlier. The Exile continued – and continues – to be seen as a watershed in Jewish history. As a people they should have died out just like the old Kingdom of Israel had. They didn't. Why not?

One reason was to be found in the sheer heroism of certain individuals. They had refused to deny their God. It was faith in God which had saved the Jews in the past.

Whether or not this incident of the fiery furnace is based on a historical incident no one can tell. It had doubtless circulated orally for some time. In the midst of the Maccabean crisis it appears to have been brought out again, used as a great example of loyalty and then written down in the form in which we now have it. The truth factor is to be seen in the Maccabeans. Their survival and eventual victory over the forces of Antiochus was a triumph of the spirit every bit as much as a triumph of military strategy.

IDEAS FOR EXPLORING FURTHER

Faith into Action   When do people need to have faith in God and/or themselves? For example: when confronting personal fears, the unknown (NC *History*: CSU 6 – voyages of discovery), conflict or danger; or when responding to others' needs (NC *History*: CSU 4 – Second World War; scientific discoveries; CSU 3 – Victorian child labour). Read about real-life and fictional characters who overcome fear, relying on inner resources (e.g. *The Owl Who Was Afraid of the Dark*, by J. Tomlinson; *I Am David*, by A. Holm; *The Village by the Sea*, by Anita Desai). Discuss starting/changing schools, joining a club, trying a new sport. Design a poster conveying helpful advice. (NC *Technology*; *Information Technology*)

183

44

Throw Him to the Lions

Daniel 6

At the time when the Jews were fighting the Greeks they began to collect together lots of stories of the old heroes. The favourite of these was Daniel. Daniel had lived in Babylon when the Jews were captives there. All the stories showed how the Jews must be ready to die for what they believed and that God would save them in the end. The story of Daniel and the lions is one of those stories.

Daniel was a bright and very clever young man. Like Joseph many hundreds of years before, he had the power to tell the meaning of dreams.

King Darius the Persian ruled over Babylon. He liked Daniel so much that he made him a governor. The other governors were all Babylonians and they were jealous of Daniel because he was more clever than any of them. They saw that Daniel was the King's favourite. They decided to get rid of him.

One day they went to the King's palace. They asked to see Darius. 'O King, live for ever,' they said. 'You are the greatest king in all the earth. We think you should be worshipped like a god.'

'What a good idea,' replied Darius. 'What shall we do about it?'

'Make an order,' said the governors. 'Say that nobody is allowed to worship anything or anybody except yourself. Then you will find out who is really loyal.'

'All right,' said the King. 'Bring a scribe and I shall do it.'

The scribe came and wrote down the order. The King signed it. As he did so he said, 'I sign this according to the customs of the Medes and Persians. That means that nothing at all can change it.'

The governors went away feeling very pleased. They knew that Daniel was a Jew. He would not obey the new law, so they would keep watch on him.

Daniel was very unhappy when he heard about the new law, but he did not hide. Three times a day, every day, he did what he had always done. He opened the window of his house which faced towards Jerusalem, knelt down and said his prayers aloud to God.

The Babylonians hid near his window. They heard every word he said. Then they hurried off to see King Darius.

'It is about the new law which you made,' they said. 'Did you not sign an order that people must worship only you and no one else? Did you not also say that it was a law of the Medes and Persians? It cannot be changed for anybody.'

'I did,' replied the King. 'Why, who has dared to break one of my laws? He shall die. I shall throw him to the lions, whoever he is.'

'It is the Jew, Daniel,' came the reply. 'He goes on praying to his own God every day. We have heard him.'

King Darius was very upset. He knew Daniel was the best governor he had ever had. He knew too that he had been tricked. But what could he do? He had made a law. It could not be changed.

Daniel was arrested and brought to the King. 'May your God set you free,' said Darius, 'but under my new law I have to throw you to the lions.'

Daniel was taken away and pushed into the lions' den. It was like a huge cave. A large stone was rolled across the entrance. It was sealed. Soldiers were put on guard. Daniel was left inside.

King Darius went back to his palace. He did not sleep all night. As soon as it was light he called for his chariot and

185

drove back to the lions' den. He stood outside and called out 'Daniel, Daniel'.

There was no answer except the roar of the lions inside.

He called again, 'Daniel, Daniel.'

The lions roared again.

Then faintly the King heard another noise. It was the voice of Daniel, as if he had just woken up.

'O King, live for ever,' it said. 'My God has kept me safe. The lions have not touched me.'

The King called to the soldiers who were on guard. They broke the seal and rolled back the stone. Daniel walked out blinking in the bright sunlight. He knelt down before the King.

Daniel and the King drove back to the palace together. The King gave another order. 'Bring to me all those governors who spoke against Daniel,' he said.

When they came in the governors were astonished to see Daniel sitting beside the King. They began to shake with fear.

'Take them away,' ordered the King. 'The lions must be getting very hungry. Give them these governors to eat instead of Daniel.' Then he turned to Daniel and said, 'Today I shall make a new order. It will say, "All people in my kingdom shall kneel to Daniel's God. He is a God who lives for ever. His kingdom shall never be destroyed. He rescues people and works wonders."'

ABOUT THE STORY

This story is to be seen in exactly the same context as the previous one. It introduces the legendary hero figure of Daniel himself.

There are two aspects of this story worth noting. The first is the idea of totally inflexible rules. The phrase 'the law of the Medes and Persians' has traditionally been used to indicate a regulation which could not be changed under any circumstances at all.

The second is a ruler who wants to become a god and be worshipped. The idea of the divine right of kings dominated Europe for centuries, and in our own times it has not entirely disappeared.

Put together, these two things always lead to diaster for someone. Daniel's courage within this story consists of suffering the consequences and thereby showing up the evil for what it is. In the circumstances the only other option would have been to run away and let the evil continue unchallenged.

IDEAS FOR EXPLORING FURTHER

Flexibility to Meet Change   Should laws be fixed for ever or do they need to change with the times? Consider changes that have occurred in your locality or compare another era of history with today. What sorts of past laws might be totally inappropriate now, especially because of modern technology and inventions (e.g. Victorian factory regulations, laws about horses). (NC *History*) Was the inflexibility of Darius a form of arrogance?

45

A Dream of Monsters and the Ancient of Days

Daniel 7: 1–14

Of all the stories of Daniel and the other heroes of the past, nothing meant more to Judas the Hammerer and his men than the story of Daniel's Vision.

'Tell it again,' they would say to the story-teller. Then they would gather round in the dusk, the light of the fire flickering on their faces. As the shadows of the hills around them darkened and turned to night the story-teller's voice alone would break the silence.

Daniel had a dream. He stood by the sea-shore. It was a dark and windy night. The wind seemed to come from all directions. It churned up the sea like a boiling cauldron. As he watched, Daniel saw something move in the middle of the water. It was a monster coming up out of the sea – no, not one, but two, three, four monsters, all different.

As Daniel watched, the first monster rose up clear of the waves. It was like a lion except that on its back it had wings like an eagle. It flew up into the air when, suddenly, the wings seemed to be plucked off and it fell to the land. There it stood on two legs like a man unable to move.

The second monster was like a huge bear. It came out of the water on its side. As its head appeared Daniel could see bones, like a man's ribs, sticking out of its mouth. Its teeth crunched into them and then it lumbered away looking for more people to eat.

The third monster appeared, looking like a leopard. Its movements were sleek and fast. It rose smoothly out of the water. Daniel could see that, like the lion, it had wings on its back. It ran like a leopard and soared like an eagle. As it came towards him Daniel saw that it had four heads. It looked in all directions at once. Nothing could take it by surprise. Then suddenly it disappeared. It vanished into the night as quickly as it had come.

Only the fourth monster was left. But it was so terrifying that Daniel could hardly describe it. It was like nothing he had ever seen before, a great ugly mass of muscle and strength, with teeth of iron which bit into everything. It spat out the pieces as it moved and then trampled them into the ground with its clumsy misshapen feet. Its head was covered in horns – ten of them. Then as Daniel watched in horror, another little horn appeared and started to grow. Three of the ten horns fell out and Daniel could see that the new horn had tiny beady eyes and a mouth. The monster came on. Nothing could stop it.

Suddenly Daniel looked upwards. The sky, which had been dark, had cleared. In the light he saw a kingly palace. A figure in white robes sat on a throne which seemed to be made of moving flames. It was The Ancient of Days. As Daniel watched, thousands of people came to bow down before him. He began to read from a large book. Daniel was spellbound.

Suddenly he remembered the monster. Where was it? He looked around. Nothing moved. The terrible creature was dead. It lay on its side melting away, as harmless as a piece of rubbish on a fire.

Daniel raised his eyes again to look at the vision in the sky. The Ancient of Days was no longer sitting alone. Another figure was standing by the fiery throne. The Ancient of Days was pointing to the earth and speaking to him. 'Go,' he was saying. 'Take control of peoples and nations. Serve them and they will serve you for ever. You are the Son of Man.'

The story-teller stopped. The group of men around the fire

189

stayed silent. In the darkness they gripped their swords more tightly. All around them the night was black. Far, far away in the distance the lights of Jerusalem flickered. Their enemy was there – the hated Antiochus, the Greek, who tortured their people and destroyed their faith. He was really the fourth monster – they knew that. The Assyrians, the Babylonians and the Persians had come and gone. Antiochus seemed more horrible than all of them. But they would win. The Temple candles would blaze with light again some day. God would be worshipped. He was greater than any monster. When would he come and save them? When would he send the Son of Man? Perhaps it would be soon. They did not know. They could only wait and make sure that they and their children were ready.

ABOUT THE STORY

The last story in this section returns us to dreams and visions. Not only do we need examples from the past to keep us going when times are hard. We need a vision of the future as well.

This dream of Daniel is weird but since Freud and Jung we have come to recognize the symbolic nature of this sort of picture and the sort of truth it contains.

The first three monsters in the dream represent the first three conquerors of God's people. First, the Assyrians had come and conquered Israel, taking away the ten northern tribes, who were never to be heard of again. At the time the Assyrian Empire had seemed all powerful but it had collapsed. Secondly, Babylon had conquered Judah and taken the people into exile. That had seemed like the end of everything but that empire too had faded away and the Jews had survived. Thirdly, the Persian Empire had swept into power and had seemed invincible. Then, suddenly, that too had gone.

Now there were the Greeks. Divided up into various groups (the ten horns) the Greek Empire seemed the greatest threat of all. The Jews were now faced not just with a physical threat but with a direct challenge to their beliefs and culture. This could really destroy them like nothing else had done. Antiochus is not a pretty picture.

The vision, however, is that he too will melt away. Israel's God is still there, breaking through the clouds and about to redeem his people.

This vision is apocalyptic – concerned with the last things. The God of all time (the Ancient of Days) will be represented in a new figure (the Son of Man). Israel will be reborn.

IDEAS FOR EXPLORING FURTHER

Myths and Legends   Read some of the Roman, Viking, Greek or Aztec myths and legends. (■ History: CSUs 1, 4, 5) What images or names are used to denote the power of the gods and their particular qualities? Think about how these images and qualities seem to differ from how Jews, Christians, Muslims, Hindus, Sikhs or Buddhists envisage the transcendent spirit/God. See Stories 35 and 41.

The Power of God   The Jews believed that God could overcome any evil. Daniel's monster represented the most terrible problem he could think of and God overcame it. Ask children to draw/model/list the most enormous problems or difficulties they can think of, or to design their own monster to represent total evil. Discuss whether religious believers might feel that God would conquer all. Would believers feel that prayer had a role to play here and that God might want us to help in the battle?

46

Adam and Eve,
or,
'What Must It Have Been Like to Have Lived at the Beginning of the World?'

Genesis 2: 5–25

Have you ever wondered what it must have been like to be alive at the very beginning of things? Nobody can tell because, of course, nobody was there to write it down at the time. But people have always wondered.

If you were the first person on the earth, how would you behave? There would be no one to tell you what to do. Everything would be perfect. Would you be perfect too?

One of the first stories in the Bible is about these questions. It may be about lots of other questions as well. The Jews thought it had lots of meanings in it. But they also enjoyed it. So can we.

Long, long ago, when God first made the earth, it had no life on it. There was no rain, so there were no trees, no grass, no flowers. There were no people either. Everything was bare and dry and empty.

One day God said to himself, 'I think I shall make a human being.' So he took some clay and squeezed it into a lump. Then he breathed on it and it came alive. It had a body, a head, two arms and two legs, and it moved about.

'Hullo, Adam,' said God. (He called it Adam because that was the word for clay.)

'Hullo,' replied Adam.

Adam looked at himself. He looked at his arms and his legs and his body. He breathed a big breath. He liked what he saw; he liked what he felt. He thought to himself, I'm half made out of the earth and I'm half made out of God. That's good. That's how it should be.

Adam looked around. It really wasn't a very nice world. There was nothing in it.

But God was still busy. Away to the east he was making a beautiful garden. The grass there was as green as green could be. The trees were tall; the flowers were full of colour. In the middle of the garden were two special trees. One was called the Tree of Life. The other was called the Tree of Knowledge.

'Come over here, Adam,' called God. 'Come and live in my garden. You can look after it for me.'

'It's very nice,' said Adam, looking around. 'In fact it's perfect. I think we will call it the Garden of Eden, the Perfect Place.'

'It's all yours,' said God. 'But just one small thing.'

'What's that?' asked Adam.

'That Tree of Knowledge,' answered God. 'You mustn't touch it. You can touch anything else and you can eat anything else but don't go near that. It's very dangerous and you might die if you eat fruit off that tree.'

'All right,' said Adam. 'Oh, there's just one thing.'

'Yes?' asked God.

'Well, I hardly like to mention it, but – well, I'm a bit lonely, that's all.'

'Oh, I can soon do something about that,' said God.

He set to work again. 'There you are,' he said at last. 'Give some names to all those.'

Adam looked around. There were lions and tigers, elephants and kangaroos, cats and dogs, snakes and every other animal you could think of. It took a long time to give them all names.

When he had finished, Adam sat down. It was nice to have all the animals. They didn't scare him. He knew all their names; they didn't know his. So he was the master.

God spoke again. 'Is everything all right now?' he asked.

'Well ...' Adam began. He paused.

'What's the matter?'

'Well, animals are all right. But I was rather hoping I could have a real mate – a bit like myself, if you know what I mean?'

'Oh, very well,' said God.

God put Adam into a deep sleep. Then he cut him open and took out one of his ribs. He healed up the wound again. God took the rib and squeezed it and pulled it into shape. When he had finished he stood it up. It was a woman. God breathed on her. She came to life.

'Wake up, Adam,' called God, 'and come over here.'

'Now that's more like it,' said Adam. 'Where did she come from?'

'I made her from one of your ribs,' said God. 'This is woman. Her name is Eve.'

Adam and Eve looked at each other. They didn't have any clothes on, but it didn't matter. There was nothing wrong. Adam and Eve didn't know about some things being good and other things being bad. Everything was just all right.

It was a happy world and it seemed that it would last for ever.

NOTES

ABOUT THE STORY

The following five stories have been put at the end simply to make the point that they are not history. They are more important than that. They belong to any age. They are not about particular individuals but about all people everywhere. They tell us what we are like as human beings and invite a response. They represent deep Jewish insights into the nature of the human condition and our relationship to the whole created order of things.

Because these stories have often been treated as if they were intended as historical accounts they have frequently been dismissed out of hand as untrue. But the important question is not 'Are they true?' It is 'Do they contain truth?' (see Introduction).

To treat these first two stories as if they are historical accounts of how the world was made is to invite all sorts of nonsense questions like: 'Should Adam have a navel?' (asked by many medieval Italian artists), 'Who did Cain and Abel marry?', 'Could snakes talk?' Rather we should be asking questions like 'If we had no heredity (i.e. we couldn't blame our parents or our upbringing) and a perfect environment ("Garden of Eden" means "paradise" or "perfection") would we be faultless?', 'How responsible are we for our own actions?', 'Why is it easier to be bad than good?', 'Who do we blame?'

The phrase 'Adam and Eve' in Hebrew has something of the connotation of 'Tom, Dick and Harry' in English. 'Adam' is also a play on the Hebrew word *adamah* meaning 'ground' or 'clay'. He comes to life when spirit is breathed into him. Humans are of the earth but also of eternal spirit. The story suggests we are responsible for our own wrongdoing. Is that true?

The place of Eve is the most difficult to accept today. To tell the story as it stands is to convey what many would regard as sexist values. Nor is it legitimate to pretend otherwise. It is not insignificant that the feminist organization Spare Rib takes its name from a stark image in this very story. However, Jewish tradition is for argument with the text, not for automatic bland acceptance and perhaps it is best to treat it in this way.

IDEAS FOR EXPLORING FURTHER

The Earth as a Home   Our planet is a home for people and animals. Find out about animal habitats. What could threaten them? What could threaten the planet as a whole? Discuss free will, the choices people make and the values behind them. Find out more about the different kinds of landscapes to be found on the earth. Link up with NC *Geography*: ATs 3, 5; *Environmental Education*; *Economic and Industrial Understanding*. Design a 'new animal' and given reasons for the design chosen.

Men and Women   Does it matter whether man or woman was created first? Is the story suggesting that human beings are at the beginning and end of creation as essential threads in the whole fabric? Is another interpretation that man and woman were made from the same lump of clay, with differences planned by God, and were meant to live together? Should each therefore respect the other, since they are complementary like two sides of a coin? (NC *Science*: genetics and evolution)

47

In the Garden of Eden, or, 'Do We Always Have to Spoil Things?'

Genesis 2: 25 – 3: 24

Adam and Eve were the first two people on earth in the last story. Everything was just right. The Garden of Eden where they lived was perfect. Could anything spoil it? The story continues. . . .

The cleverest animal in the garden was the snake. It slid across the grass and spoke to Eve. 'It's a nice garden, isn't it?' he said.

'Yes,' replied Eve. 'That's why it's called "The Garden of Eden". It means "Paradise".'

'A pity you can't eat the fruit off the trees,' said the snake. 'Of course,' he went on, 'it doesn't bother me. I don't eat fruit. But it must be hard for you, seeing all those lovely juicy peaches and pears and not being able to touch them.'

'Oh, but we can,' cried Eve. 'We can eat the fruit off all the trees, except that one in the middle. God told us to leave that one alone. He said we might die if we ate the fruit off that tree.'

The snake laughed. 'He would, wouldn't he?' he said.

'What do you mean?' said Eve.

'Well, that's the Tree of Knowledge. If you eat that fruit you'll know everything. Then you would be as clever as God himself. Just think of that. *You* could be God. Go on, have a bite.'

Eve looked at the tree. It did look tempting. She reached out a hand. Then she drew it back. No, she couldn't. The snake laughed again, a nasty, sneering laugh which said, 'You daren't, you're frightened'. She looked at the tree again. Her arm reached out and her fingers touched the fruit. It came away in her hand. For a moment she held it, looking at it. Then with a sudden movement she put it to her mouth and took a large bite. It tasted delicious.

Eve turned and ran back to where Adam was. 'Taste this,' she said, holding out the fruit.

Adam took a bite without asking what it was. Then they looked at one another.

Suddenly everything felt different. They both felt shy.

Eve spoke first. 'Why do you keep walking around with nothing on?' she said. 'You look disgusting. For goodness' sake go and cover yourself up.'

'You can talk,' said Adam angrily.

They started to argue and be nasty to one another. All of a sudden the garden didn't seem a very nice place any more.

The hot day started to come to an end. A cool breeze blew. The evening was the best time of the day. God walked through the garden. Adam and Eve heard him coming. They hid in the bushes.

'Adam!' called God. 'Adam, where are you? Oh, there you are,' he went on as he saw Adam behind a tree. 'What are you doing there?'

'Well, I heard you coming,' said Adam quickly, 'and as I hadn't got any clothes on – well – it's not very nice, is it? I mean, I didn't want you to catch me all naked, did I?'

There was a silence. When God spoke again his voice was both sad and angry. 'What has made you think it's wrong?' he asked. 'Have you been eating from that tree – the one I told you not to touch?'

197

'It's not my fault,' Adam said, crying. Pointing at Eve, he said, 'It was her. She made me do it.'

'Oh no, it wasn't,' shouted Eve, coming out from behind another bush. 'You keep blaming me. I couldn't help it. It was all the snake's fault.'

Adam and Eve started to argue again.

'Stop!' roared God. 'It is too late now. You have spoilt it all. You could have taken the fruit off the Tree of Life. I offered you that. Then you could have lived for ever. You were free to choose to be on my side or to go against me. You are stupid. You cannot stay in my garden any more. You will have to go and live outside. You will have to work very hard there. Nothing is growing at all. But it is your own fault. Go on, off you go.'

Adam and Eve crept out of the garden. The snake followed them. God was right. It was their own fault. Would people always be as stupid as they had been?

NOTES

ABOUT THE STORY

This is a continuation of the Adam and Eve story, divided up here only because of length. In this section the predominant theme is that of the coming of evil into the world.

Experience has shown that if this story is simply told straight it is perfectly acceptable and clearly understood by young children. In form it is very like similar stories from other religions such as the Hindu story of Rama and Sita. There is only one thing that Adam and Eve are not allowed to do, that is, to pick the apples. Every five-year-old knows that that is exactly what they will want to do.

In our own culture it is older children who may experience more difficulty. They may already have been educated out of being able to appreciate this traditional way of communicating moral values. In the same way teachers sometimes have to accept that children do not always have the difficulties adults experience with this sort of material. It is possible to be too rational.

Children who, after listening to and acting out this story, can be heard in the playground accusing one another of 'having the snake' or 'biting the apple' have probably understood it far better than university professors who journey to the eastern Mediterranean to locate the site of the Garden of Eden!

It is interesting to note that even in this early tradition self-consciousness is linked with nakedness.

IDEAS FOR EXPLORING FURTHER

Good and Bad   List all the symbols you can think of associated with good and bad: animals, plants, etc. Is one list much longer than the other? Why? Refer to children's stories, nursery rhymes, folk tales, etc., for similar material. Older children could act out the struggle between good and evil as represented in other cultures (e.g. the Hindu Ramayana).

Clothes   What does our choice of clothes tell other people about us? How do they express our personalities? Why do we invent uniforms? Discuss clothes worn by priests and members of religious communities. Do the colours and styles have significance? Invite a representative of a religious tradition to explain the clothing worn on particular occasions. What about clothes for baptism, services of initiation, marriage and festivals?

Stories   Find examples of stories which are true and stories which carry truths. With older pupils, look at traditional tales meant for very young children. Can they be understood at more than one level? See Stories 41 and 48.

48

Noah and the Flood, or, 'Why Doesn't God Get Rid of Evil?'

Genesis 6: 5 – 9: 21

It was very funny. People laughed and laughed. Every day more and more came to see and join in the fun. They could hardly believe their eyes. Old man Noah was building a boat. And what a boat! It was huge, a hundred and fifty metres long, twenty-five metres wide and about fifteen metres tall. It was more like a row of houses than a boat. Noah called it his Ark.

If it had been near the sea it might have made sense. But Noah lived a long, long way from the sea. In fact, he was right on the edge of the desert. Old Noah was quite mad but he didn't seem to mind people laughing at him. Every day he went on hammering away.

Far from minding the laughter, Noah felt very sorry for the people. They wouldn't be laughing much longer. Not if God were right – and he'd never been wrong before. It had all started when God had called him.

'Noah,' God had said.

'Yes, God,' Noah answered. 'What is it?'

'I am beginning to wish I had never made people,' said God. 'They are all so horrible and they keep trying to take my world away from me. It was a good world when it started. Now it is all dirty and it wants washing clean. But there are one or two good things in it. I do not want to wash them away and they include you, so listen carefully.'

Noah listened very carefully while God told him exactly what he had to do.

That's why he was spending all this time building his Ark. Now it was nearly finished. He looked up at the sky. Not a cloud in sight. He shrugged his shoulders. Never mind, it was time to get everything on board. He went off for his wife.

'Come on, come on, there's not much time.'

The crowd roared with laughter as Noah tried to push his fat wife up the gangplank.

'I don't want to live in this silly boat,' she screamed. 'They're right,' she went on, pointing to the crowd, 'you've gone stark raving mad.'

Noah took no notice. He got her inside. Then he said, 'I'm just going for the boys.'

Noah's sons Shem, Ham and Japheth were grown up. They had wives of their own. Noah brought them all back and made them go into the Ark as well. 'Now for the animals,' he said.

'Oh, no,' groaned his wife, 'you're not serious.'

'Oh yes, I am,' answered Noah, and off he went into the forest.

A little while later he came back leading the strangest procession anyone had ever seen. There were two of everything, a bull and a cow, a cockerel and a hen, a lion and a lioness – hundreds of different kinds of animals and birds.

'Where are you going to put all that lot?' asked Noah's wife in despair.

'I've made three decks,' replied Noah. 'We will live upstairs – they can all go down below.'

He pushed and prodded the animals up into the Ark. Then he closed the door.

The crowd of people outside were still laughing but the weather had turned cloudy and it started to rain so they all went home. Next day it was still raining. It rained and it rained. The sky went black; the wind blew hard. It had never rained like this before. It went on and on, day after day. The rivers filled up. Then they overflowed into the fields. Houses got washed away. The floods got deeper and deeper.

Suddenly old Noah's Ark gave a shudder. It moved. The water was so deep it was floating. The land was all covered with water. The Ark floated away across a silent world. No one was laughing or crying now. Everything had gone deathly quiet. Inside the Ark there was still plenty of life, but outside everything was quiet and dead. The water even covered the mountain tops.

It stopped raining. The Ark floated on and on. There was no land to be seen anywhere.

The food we have won't last for ever, thought Noah. He was getting worried. He opened the window and looked out. There was nothing except water as far as the eye could see.

Noah went down below where the animals were. He picked out a dove and took it upstairs. He held it in his hands outside the window and threw it into the air.

The dove flew away. Noah waited. High up into the sky it flew in a great circle. Then it dropped down again and landed on the Ark. Noah let it in and shut the window.

He waited for a week. Then once again he took the dove and threw it out of the window. Again it soared into the air, but this time it flew off out of sight. Noah waited. Nothing happened. In the end he went back inside.

That evening as he was having supper Noah heard a small noise. He rushed up on to the deck. There stood the dove. In its beak it held a twig with leaves on it. Noah danced for joy. 'Land, land!' he shouted. 'The dove has found a living tree.' But he still couldn't see it.

Another week passed. Noah sent the dove out again. It never came back. In the middle of the night the Ark shook again. It had grounded. By next morning the flood had soaked away. The Ark was sitting in the middle of dry ground again.

Everybody was very happy. Noah opened the doors. People and animals rushed out. The wild animals dashed off into the forest. Noah and his sons began to make a plough.

202

Noah ploughed the land and became a farmer. He made a beautiful vineyard. When harvest time came he gathered in all the grapes. He made them into wine. It was a good world again, now that all the bad people had been washed away. It was time to celebrate. Noah drank some of his wine. It was very good. He felt happy and he went on drinking. He drank and he drank until he got very drunk and started to do silly things.

Up in heaven God sighed. 'Here we go again,' he said to himself.

NOTES

ABOUT THE STORY

It seems futile to speculate on whether or not there was a flood of huge proportions in the ancient world. There may well have been several. But this is an ethical and theological story before it is a historical one.

Its theme is simple but profound. The world is potentially good. It is human beings who introduce evil. It appears that the only way to remove evil is to remove people, or at least to start again with just the good ones, who are very thin on the ground. History shows many examples of this desire for a 'final solution'. (See also Stories 17 and 30.)

The flood is the device for cleansing. Only Noah is in close enough harmony with God to hear the warning call. His goodness saves the world of living things. By contrast with humans, animals are innocent but helpless. They depend for their survival or destruction on the behaviour of people.

As with the story of Jonah there is a tendency to cut this story short and, in doing so, to miss the crucial point. There are no perfect human beings. Noah, for all his goodness, is flawed. When the crisis is over and the flood has abated his sons find him comatose with drunkenness, lying naked in his tent. They literally do a cover-up job in an attempt to hide his failings.

The key question to this, as to so many other stories in this collection, is not so much 'Did it happen?' as 'Does it happen?' Are human beings like this? Do we constantly yearn to start all over again? Can the world be saved from the disaster brought about by human failing?

IDEAS FOR EXPLORING FURTHER

Renewal   Talk about times when people are given second chances, opportunities to begin again. What sort of New Year's resolutions do people make? Are they kept? Discuss the role of water in baptism as a sign of cleansing, forgiveness and acceptance. Talk about periods in different religious calendars when people try to repent and start again (e.g. Lent, the Day of Atonement, Ramadan). Talk about pilgrimages and retreats as part of a process of renewal. (Cf. Stories 5, 31, the Hindu story of Manu's Ark, in *Stories from the Hindu World*, by Jamila Gavin and Joanna Troughton, Simon & Schuster.)

Conservation   See Story 46. Make links with NC *Geography*: AT 5; *Environmental Education*; *Science* – processes of life.

Music   Play parts of 'Mr Noah' (published by Cassell) and/or 'Noye's Fludde', by Benjamin Britten. Compose or select music to accompany the story acted out through children's drama, puppets, prose or poetry.

Art   Use a variety of colours and techniques to convey the different emotions water can arouse in people (e.g. peace, excitement, foreboding, terror).

Truth   See notes on Stories 16, 41, 46, 47.

49

The Story of Job,
or,
'Why Is It That Bad Things Happen to Good People?'

The Book of Job

Sometimes life seems very unfair. People who are greedy and selfish often get rich. Other people who are honest and kind sometimes get laughed at. Then there are accidents and illnesses and we think, Why does it have to happen to me? I haven't done anything wrong.

Long ago people used to believe that if you were very poor or sick or crippled it was because you had done something wrong. The Jews knew that was not true. God wasn't like that. They tried to show it in a story about a man called Job. It has become one of the most famous stories in the world. The story of Job was first told as a very long poem. We shall have to try and tell it as a short, simple story.

Once upon a time there lived a very rich man called Job. He had a wife and ten children, seven sons and three daughters. They were all very happy and nobody minded that Job was the richest man for miles around. He deserved to be. He was a good man. Everybody liked him.

Up in heaven God was having a meeting with some of his leading angels. One of the most important angels was what we would call the Inspector-General. He was known as the Satan. His job was to keep an eye on things and to make sure that everything was as it should be. He was very strict and he didn't like people very much.

'Tell me what you have been doing,' said God to the Satan.

'Oh, I've been wandering around,' he replied, 'just watching people. You can't take your eyes off them, you know. They are never as good as they look. You've got to watch them all the time.'

'Not all of them,' replied God. 'Look at Job. He is the best sort of person, always loyal. You can trust him anywhere.'

'Of course,' said the Satan. 'But then, he's lucky. He's rich, he's got a good wife, ten children and everything is fine. It's easy for him to be good. Take it all away from him and he will be just like everyone else.'

God thought for a minute. Then he said, 'You are wrong. You put Job to the test. You will soon find that his being good has nothing to do with all his riches.'

The Satan smiled nastily and went off. Down on earth he found Job and his wife at home. All their children were away at a party. The Satan set to work.

Job was sitting peacefully when a messenger burst in. 'You're ruined,' he shouted. 'Raiders have attacked your herdsmen. They have killed them all and driven away your horses, cattle and sheep.'

Before anyone could say anything another messenger dashed in. 'Help!' he called. 'Wild tribesmen from the desert have stolen all your camels and killed the drivers.'

A third messenger arrived. His news was worst of all. The tears ran down his cheeks. 'Your children,' he sobbed. 'They're all dead. A hurricane hit the house where the party was taking place. The walls fell down. Everyone inside has been killed.'

By now everyone was screaming and crying – everyone, that is, except Job. He had knelt down. His prayer could be heard.

'O God,' he said, 'when I came into the world I had nothing.

206

When I die I can't take anything with me. You give, you take away. I shall always trust you.'

Up in heaven God smiled. He was right. Job had passed the test. He was an even better man now than he had been before. The Satan had failed.

The Satan wasn't smiling when he came back. 'It wasn't much of a test, was it?' he said. 'You let me hurt Job himself and he will soon curse you. They all do.'

'Job will not,' replied God. 'Try your hardest – as long as you do not kill him. He will even use your tortures to become a good man.'

The Satan went off again. This time he covered Job with sores and boils. Job was as miserable as he could be. He itched all over. He couldn't sleep; he couldn't rest. His wife screamed at him, 'How can you still believe in God after all this?'

'What a thing to say,' Job replied. 'It's no good just loving God when life is easy. We have to take life as it comes.'

But all Job's friends were like his wife. They came to him one after another. 'You must have done something really bad,' said one.

'But I haven't,' replied Job, 'I am just the same as I have always been.'

His friends shook their heads and went away.

Job was all alone. He felt very sad. What have I done to deserve this? he thought. I used to be happy. I have always tried to help other people, but look at me now. People used to stand up when I came along. They thought I was important when I was on the Council. Now even the young people laugh at me when I go down the street. Why does God treat people like this?

Up in heaven God could hear Job. He spoke to him directly.

'You are a man,' God said. 'How much do you really know? Where were you when the earth was made? Who created the stars of the morning? Where were you when the mighty seas tumbled out from the earth? Have you been down in the deepest parts of the ocean or flown up among the stars? How old are you alongside the mountains and the valleys? Why do people think that they are at the centre of the universe?'

'You are right,' said Job. 'Really, I am so small. My problems seem very big to me, but I am such a tiny part of the universe. When I look around at everything I see my troubles for what they really are. I have said too much. I am sorry.'

The Satan had failed. Job was a good man even when things were hard for him. He had learned through suffering. It hadn't made him all bitter.

Job's sores vanished. He became wealthy again. He started another family and he lived to be a very old man.

NOTES

ABOUT THE STORY

Once again we need to remember that these are Jewish stories. From the earliest days most rabbis have seen the story of Job as wholly fictional. In that way it poses deep questions about the nature of human beings and the nature of God.

The Book of Job stands all on its own. It is timeless in that it does not appear to belong to any particular age or place. It has always been seen as a book of wisdom. It is part of the genius of the Jewish people that, for them, philosophy is never abstract. The arguments take place, within stories, between colourfully drawn characters, both human and divine. Hyperbole is used to make contrasts. Job doesn't just suffer; he is totally devastated.

This story introduces Satan. Note that, while he is deeply cynical about human nature, he is not presented in this story as the embodiment of evil itself. He is a sort of prosecuting counsel, allowed to test out his theory that all humans are corrupt at heart.

The central question is that of suffering. In contrast to popular belief (not by any means absent today) that suffering was largely the fault of those who suffered, this story seems to suggest that suffering is less of an effect than a cause. It comes upon anyone but when it comes it shows up a person's real character.

There is a social dimension too. At the beginning of the story Job is rich. It is suggested that because of this he can hide his true character in a way that the poor and the disadvantaged cannot. To find out what he is really like it is necessary to reduce his circumstances to those of utter misfortune.

The story is careful to avoid any suggestion that God causes suffering but accepts that he allows it. This story gives no particular answers but it explores all the questions. This surely makes it rich in educational terms.

IDEAS FOR EXPLORING FURTHER

Suffering   Make links with Stories 9 (seeking God's strength), 23 (courage) and 35 (hope). Talk about how suffering can change people's character for the better or worse. Cf. *Pollyanna*, by Eleanor H. Porter, where Pollyanna invents 'The Glad Game'; *What Katy Did*, by S. Coolidge, where a back injury teaches Katy many lessons; *The Water Babies*, by C. Kingsley, where Tom finally triumphs over his ills; *Charlie's House*, by R. Schermbrucker, where Charlie shows resourcefulness in South Africa; *What's It Like to Be Me?*, compiled by disabled children; *Spellhorn*, by Berlie Doherty, about an adventurous blind girl.

Temptation   Cf. Story 47. Draw symbols of evil and indicate on them occasions when children, or others, have been tempted. Let older pupils hear excerpts from *The Screwtape Letters*, by C. S. Lewis. How can we combat temptation? Does it help to consider that others might be hurt or upset?

Job   For each misery befalling Job, ask a group of pupils to pretend they are one of Job's neighbours wishing to tell others about the latest event. Make a tape or write down what this neighbour will say. Report on Job's feelings, thoughts about God, memories and hopes. Combine the scripts (or ad lib within the basic framework) to make a play. (NC *English*: ATs 1, 3)

50

Living in God's Way,
or,
'Who Is Really Important?'

Ecclesiasticus 38: 25–39

We have come to the end of our stories. Together they make up one big story. It is the story of how one group of people came to know God and to pass on what they learned to us.

The ancient Hebrews, Israelites and Jews weren't always very clever or sensible. In fact sometimes, just like the rest of us, they were very stupid, but they never gave up their faith in God completely.

At other times they could be very wise. Some of the wisest things they ever said were made into poems. We will finish with one of those pieces of poetry. It was first written in Hebrew, the language of the Jews.

It is a poem about ordinary people. God usually works through ordinary people. Again and again the prophets who were farmers and peasants had to try to rescue the Israelites and the Jews from the silly things that kings and rulers were doing.

This poem tells how the really important people in the world are those who live close to God and close to the world He created:

> The farmer
> ploughing the field, proud of his goad,
> driving his oxen, lost to the world,
> talking, talking of cattle,
> following the furrow by day,
> fattening the heifers by night.

The blacksmith
sitting by his anvil in a world of pig-iron,
scorched by the forge, fighting the furnace
    heat,
deafened by hammers' din, rapt in his pattern,
firm to finish his work, fashioning it into the
    night.

The potter
working at his wheel, turning it with his feet,
lost in his task of making up his tally,
slapping and puddling his clay,
engrossed in his glazing,
staying awake cleaning out his kiln.

These men trust in their hands;
their craftsmanship is their wisdom.
Without them cities would be empty –
nobody living there,
nobody coming and going.
You won't hear them on the City Council
or see them sitting in the Assembly;
you won't find them among the judges –
they can't make head or tail of the Law;
they don't talk like scholars –
they can't quote the critics.

Yet
they hold the world in their hands;
their worship is in their work.

It was into the family of a village carpenter that the best-known Jew of all was to be born. He was never rich, he never looked for power. But his life changed the world and began a whole new religion.

That is why it is a separate story, told as a lot of different stories in another book, just like this one.

NOTES

ABOUT THE STORY

The poem in this final section is again taken from Jewish wisdom literature, in this case from the Book of Ecclesiasticus in the Apochrypha. It is included because it raises the fundamental question for religious education of what counts as important.

'Wisdom' used to be a key word in education but it has been replaced by lesser words such as 'knowledge' and 'information'. T. S. Eliot's poem 'The Rock' contains the lines:

Where is the wisdom we have lost in knowledge?
Where is the knowledge we have lost in information?

Wisdom, in Jewish eyes, is divine. It is deeply moral, concerned with the right way to live. It does not hesitate to make value judgements but often, as here, these challenge conventional values. In this sense it is not so much indoctrinatory as prophetic and anti-indoctrinatory. It challenges us to look again at the conventional way in which we are brought up and to re-examine the normal order of things.

What this poem teaches is that those who live close to the world of nature and natural things are likely to live closest to God and to be most at peace with themselves. It also seems to suggest that it is only when we lose ourselves in some creative employment that we truly find ourselves. The way of creative work is as valid as any other way to God. However, it has to be said yet again that women are ignored and need to be reinstated. It seems an appropriate prelude to beginning the second volume of these stories with the Magnificat, which expresses similar sentiments but in rather more robust terms and from a Jewish woman's mouth.

IDEAS FOR EXPLORING FURTHER

Importance   Who do children feel are the really important people in the world? They could write a poem or story to express their ideas or each make a clay model of a really important person and combine the models to form a display. Add labels to show the children's reasons for their choice. Consider people to whom the children are important and why. Does this give them any sense of responsibility? Look for stories in sacred writings where the hero or heroine appears at some stage to be weak and unimportant (e.g. in the Bible: Ruth, Rebekah, Moses, Rahab, Samson, David, Jeremiah).

Trust and Cooperation   Is it true that if a community is to function well, then people must trust each other and cooperate? Put the children in pairs and blindfold one partner. Ask the blindfolded person to make something simple with clay while their partner helps them by giving advice, passing equipment, etc. Swop roles. Discuss how the pupils felt when they were blindfolded and not. How much did pupils have to trust each other? Can successful outcomes be achieved through cooperation?

Bibliography

Bawden, Nina *Carrie's War*, Puffin.

Bissett, E. & Palmer, M. *Worlds of Difference*, Worldwide Fund for Nature, Panda House, Godalming, Surrey GU7 1XR.

British Museum Education Service Catalogue, British Museum Education Service, Great Russell Street, London WC1B 3DG.

Coolidge, Susan *What Katy Did*, Armada.

Desai, Anita *The Village by the Sea*, Puffin.

Doherty, Berlie *Spellhorn*, Lion.

Exley, H. (ed.) *What's It Like to Be Me?* (written entirely by disabled children), Letterbox Library, 8 Bradbury Street, London N16 8JN.

Exploring Questions and *Exploring a Theme: Barriers*, Christian Education Movement, Royal Buildings, Victoria Street, Derby DE1 1GW.

Faith in Action series, RMEP.

Gavin, Jamila & Troughton, Joanna *Stories from the Hindu World*, Macdonald/Simon & Schuster.

Holm, A. *I Am David*, Magnet.

Jackson, R. & Starkings, D. (eds) *The Junior RE Handbook*, Stanley Thornes.

Jaffrey, Madhur *Seasons of Splendour: Tales, Myths and Legends of India*, Puffin.

Kingsley, Charles *The Water Babies*, Gollancz.

Kumar, Arvan *The Heartstone Odyssey*, Allied Mouse, Longden Court, Spring Gardens, Buxton, Derbyshire SK17 6BZ.

LeGuin, Ursula *The Wizard of Earthsea*, Penguin.

Lewis, C. S. *The Screwtape Letters*, Fontana/Collins.

Lewis, C. S. *The Lion, the Witch and the Wardrobe; Prince Caspian; Voyage of the Dawn Treader; The Silver Chair; A Horse and His Boy; The Magician's Nephew; The Last Battle*, Puffin.

Living Festivals series, RMEP.

Mr Noah (cassette of the musical for primary schools), Cassell.

Paton Walsh, Jill *Fireweed*, Puffin.

Porter, Eleanor H. *Pollyanna*, Puffin.

Rankin, J. *et al.* *Religious Education Topics for the Primary School*, Longman.

The Ramayana for Children, The Multicultural Education Centre, Bishop Road, Bishopston, Bristol BS7 8LS.

Sampson, Fay *Pangur Ban*, Lion.

Schermbrucker, R. *Charlie's House*, Letterbox Library, 8 Bradbury Street, London N16 8JN.

Scholefield, Lynne *Passover*, Living Festivals series, RMEP.

Stewart, Maureen *Creation Stories*, Hodder & Stoughton.

Tolkien, J. R. R. *The Hobbit*, Unwin.

Tomlinson, Jill *The Owl Who Was Afraid of the Dark*, Puffin.

Wilde, Oscar *The Selfish Giant*, Puffin.

Wilcox, Linda *Refugees*, Franklin Watts.

Note Letterbox Library, 8 Bradbury Street, London N16 8JN, specializes in non-racist, non-sexist and anti-stereotype books. Send for the catalogue.

We have listed the main themes and issues encountered in the stories and indicated the pages where these stories may be found. Page numbers in **bold** type show where ideas for exploring these themes and issues are suggested in the Notes.

214

215

216